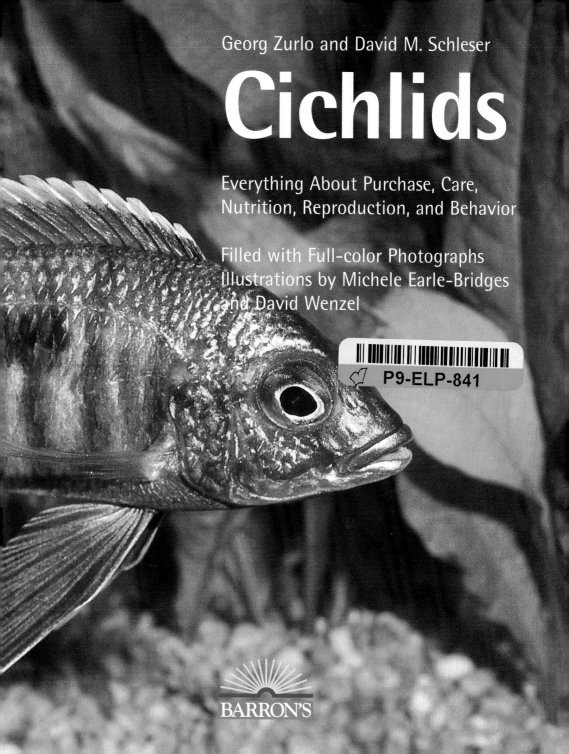

Georg Zurlo and David M. Schleser

Cichlids

Everything About Purchase, Care,
Nutrition, Reproduction, and Behavior

Filled with Full-color Photographs
Illustrations by Michele Earle-Bridges
and David Wenzel

BARRON'S

2 CONTENTS

INTRODUCTION

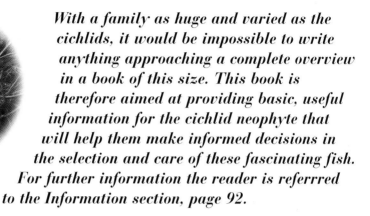

With a family as huge and varied as the cichlids, it would be impossible to write anything approaching a complete overview in a book of this size. This book is therefore aimed at providing basic, useful information for the cichlid neophyte that will help them make informed decisions in the selection and care of these fascinating fish. For further information the reader is referrred to the Information section, page 92.

The Cichlid Family

Cichlids are arguably one of the most popular families of aquarium fish. This is despite the fact that many hobbyists think of them as aggressive, bad-tempered fish that are highly intolerant of tankmates, whether they are of their own or different species, and get special delight out of destroying plants and rearranging the aquarium's architecture. Whereas this is indeed true for a segment of the cichlid family, it is by no means the rule. For example, the angelfish, *Pteryophyllum scalare*, undoubtedly the most popular of cichlids, is quite at home in a well-planted, mixed community aquarium.

*The angelfish, **Pterophyllum scalare**, in all its many domesticated forms and colors, is the most popular of all cichlids and one of the most popular aquarium fish. This fish is a marbled veiltail.*

Although a relatively small number of the larger popular cichlids, such as the Oscar (*Astronotus ocellatus*) might require solitary confinement, or be kept as a compatible pair in a roomy aquarium, most of the unpleasant experiences people have had with cichlids are the result of poor selection of species and improper housing and care.

What Are Cichlids?

With an estimated 1,000-plus species (many yet to be described) the family Cichlidae is one of the largest families of fish known. Except for a relatively few species that can tolerate brackish or even marine conditions, they are all freshwater fish. Cichlids possess certain anatomic characteristics that have caused taxonomists to group them within one family. Some of the most easily seen are a single long

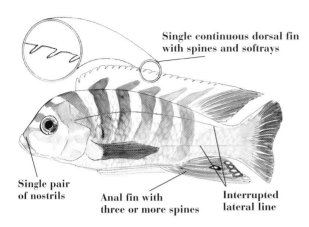

Single continuous dorsal fin
with spines and softrays

Single pair
of nostrils

Anal fin with
three or more spines

Interrupted
lateral line

*External anatomy
of a cichlid.*

*Cichlids may vary
widely in size and
shape, but all possess
common anatomic
features.*

dorsal fin comprised of both a spiny and soft portion, an anal fin with three or more spines, a lateral line that is divided into two separate sections (interrupted, or broken, lateral line), and a single, rather than paired, nostril opening on each side.

There is so much diversity of size and shape among the different species of cichlids that it is hard to believe they all belong to one family. There are giants that measure from 28 to 32 inches (70–80 cm) in length, and dwarfs that are full grown at 1½ inches (3.4 cm). Most cichlids have a "typical" fish shape, but others may be slender and spindle-shaped, deep-bodied and thick in cross section, or even tall and laterally flattened.

The vast majority of cichlids are of suitable size for the average home aquarium, beautifully colored, and exhibiting fascinating and complex courtship and breeding behaviors. Although most make hardy, long-lived, and easily satisfied aquarium inhabitants, there are others that are extremely delicate and a challenge for the most

experienced hobbyist to keep and breed. This has led to their great popularity with both the beginning and advanced aquarists. It is fair to say that there is probably a cichlid to suit the tastes of just about any aquarist.

Distribution of Cichlids

Cichlids can be found throughout most of Africa, including the island of Madagascar, the Neotropics north into south Texas, and the Indian subcontinent. Most cichlid species hail from Africa, with the vast majority of these inhabiting Lakes Malawi, Tanganyika, and Victoria in the Great Rift Valley. A few species extend this range north into parts of the Middle East. The neotropical portion of the family includes about 100 species from Mexico, Central America, and the Caribbean Islands, and well over 250 species from tropical and subtropical regions of South America. Completing this list are the three species belonging to the genus *Etroplus* that inhabit southern India and Sri Lanka.

Cichlid Classification and Latin Names

Taxonomy is the science of identifying, describing, classifying, and naming living organisms. In 1766 the Swedish naturalist Carl Linnaeus introduced the binomial nomenclature system. Ever since then every living species, whether plant or animal, has been classified this way. Every described species has been given a scientific name consisting of two italicized words written in Latin, or in a Latinized form. The first word is called the *generic name* and is always capitalized. The second part of the name is the *species* and never capitalized. Sometimes a single species may be further divided into *subspecies*, or geographical variants.

Knowing the scientific names of cichlids is important for many reasons. Many have no popular English language names, while some common names are applied to more than a single species. Knowing the scientific names permits you to refer to a cichlid with little

possibility of being misunderstood, and you will have no problems communicating with aquarists in other countries.

It sometimes becomes necessary to change a species' scientific name. This may be due in part to our increasing knowledge about its relationships or because it becomes apparent that the species in question had previously been described under a different name. These changes can be frustrating, but still must be done. Taxonomy, as with all of science, is constantly evolving.

In this book, when all or part of a cichlid's scientific name appears in quotes (such as "*Cichlasoma*" sp.) it is meant to indicate that the classification of this fish is still a matter of debate.

Worldwide distribution of the family Cichlidae.

OBTAINING YOUR CICHLIDS

Pet dealers usually have a good selection of the most popular kinds of cichlids. Private fish breeders often raise some rarer kinds. You can find the names of breeders in the classified section of aquarists' magazines.

Which Species?

Hobbyists new to keeping cichlids should look for species with the following qualities:
✔ Select fish that will not outgrow your aquarium. For example, if your aquarium has a capacity of 20 gallons (57 L), do not buy any cichlid that will grow to more than 3 inches (7.6 cm) in length. If you are fortunate to have a 100-gallon (380-L) tank you can then keep a number of fish that might grow to a length of 6 to 8 inches (15–20 cm). Buying fish that will outgrow their aquarium is one of the biggest mistakes made by beginners.
✔ Pick species that at adulthood will all be of similar size. With few exceptions small and large species will not do well together and should not be mixed in the same aquarium.

The blue ram, Microgeophagus ramirezi, is a popular but slightly delicate species generally available at pet stores.

✔ Because cichlids coming from different parts of the world frequently require very different aquarium conditions, exhibit different behaviors, and have evolved different body languages, it is strongly advised not to mix cichlids from different regions of the globe. For example, it would be a big mistake trying to keep cichlids from the African Rift Valley lakes that require hard and alkaline water with species from the soft, acidic waters found throughout much of the Amazon basin.
✔ Unless you intend to keep only one cichlid in a tank of its own as a special pet, select cichlid species that are not famous for their excessive aggressiveness toward others of their own kind, other cichlids, or other species of fish.

If you are uncertain about any of the above guidelines seek the advise of a knowledgeable pet store employee or an experienced hobbyist.

Where You Can Obtain Cichlids

Most pet stores generally stock a large variety of species, particularly those from South America and the African Rift Valley lakes.

Artificially colored, dyed, and painted fish

An increasingly common and deplorable practice is the artificial coloring of aquarium fish, mainly by Asian exporters, in order to increase their sales. Methods used include adding a coloring agent to the food that can be absorbed through the fish's gut, dyeing the fish, and actually injecting dyes into the fish. Not only are these practices inhumane, but the coloration gradually fades and disappears, leaving a normally colored specimen. At the present time the cichlids that are most often treated in this way are albino Oscars and kribensis, and the man-made hybrid known as the red parrot cichlid (photo, page 12). The last species should not be confused with the real parrot cichlid, *Hoplarchus psitticus* (*psitticus* means parrot in Latin), a large and uncommon South American species.

Dyed fish most commonly come in shades of blue, green, red, yellow, and purple, and when sold the word "painted" or "jelly-bean" usually precedes the common name of the species, such as painted Oscars, or jelly-bean parrot cichlids. If you refuse to buy any painted fish, and inform pet store owners that you will take your business elsewhere unless they stop selling artificially colored fish, we can stamp out this abhorrent practice.

Most of these have been tank raised and are well adapted to aquarium conditions and foods.

Private fish breeders are another source of cichlids, particularly the rarer, less popular, or more delicate species. Local aquarium societies are often good places to meet such breeders. You can also find them listed in the classified sections of most aquarium magazines, or in the journals of national organizations such as the American Cichlid Association (see Information, page 92). Most local and national aquarium societies have yearly conventions that include a large auction of aquarium fish, plants, and supplies. These are excellent sources of tank-raised cichlids of both common and rare varieties.

Fish Selection

1. Select immature specimens. Even though most young cichlids will not have developed their full colors, buying smaller fish has a number of advantages: Not only are they less expensive, but younger fish adjust more readily to new surroundings, and tend to get along better with each other as they mature than fish purchased as adults.

2. Select only healthy fish. Unless it is one of the few bottom-dwelling cichlids, they should be swimming around with fins well spread and not sitting in a corner with clamped fins. There should be no signs of injury or disease such as torn and frayed fins, missing scales, red sores on the body, cloudy eyes, obvious parasites, or abnormally rapid respiration.

3. Another test is to have a store employee feed them. Healthy cichlids are eager feeders. If the fish ignore the food, or spit it out, do not buy them.

4. Always avoid purchasing a cichlid whose excreta trails behind it in long, mucousy white strings. This is a classic sign of infestation by the debilitating intestinal flagellate *Hexamita* (see page 43).

Note: Watch the behavior of the fish over an extended period of time. This is the best way to judge their state of health.

Pairs Versus Groups

If your aim is to breed your cichlids, buying a small group of immature fish gives them the opportunity to naturally select compatible mates. When you buy a male and female out of a large group of adult fish there is no assurance that they will be a compatible pair, and more often than not this will *not* be the case. Instead, fights will develop as the dominant fish attempts to drive the other from its territory, which can result in the severe injury and even death of the submissive specimen. Exceptions can sometimes be made for pairs of cichlids that have already developed a pair bond. You can tell this by watching them in the dealer's tank and seeing if they stay together and actively defend the portion of the aquarium that they have selected as their territory. But even this is not without risk, as many times the pair bond will break down when the fish are moved to a different aquarium.

Sexing Cichlids

Although adult males and females of many cichlids can be separated by differences in color, fin shape, or size, this is not the case with small specimens. Telling males from females in a shoal of immature cichlids is generally difficult if not impossible. This is another reason for buying a group of about six young fish if your goal is to have at least one true pair. If this is not possible, size may be a useful clue. Males of many cichlid species grow faster than females. This fact is relevant in helping you guess the sex of small fish only if the group being offered for sale are all siblings from one spawn. If possible, you should select more females than males. This is because male cichlids are generally more aggressive than females and having more females than males will help spread out a male's aggressiveness among a number of fish, rather than to just focus his attention on one specimen. After your young fish mature and hopefully pair up you can dispose of the extra specimens to a fellow hobbyist or trade them in at your pet store.

Mixing Species

If you wish to keep a mixed cichlid aquarium or keep your cichlids with other species of fish you must be certain that they will do well together. Always bear in mind that your efforts will be more successful if your aquarium is large and roomy, rather than small and cramped.

Guidelines

Here is a list of guidelines that you should follow.

✔ Your aquarium should be large enough to accommodate all the fish at maturity.

✔ The fish should all require the same water conditions. For instance, cichlids from the soft and acidic blackwater regions of Amazonia should not be mixed with those that demand water that is hard and alkaline, such as many Central American and all African Rift Valley species. Nor should species such as the discus

The Oscar, Astronotus ocellatus, *is a large, aggressive species that will quickly outgrow a small aquarium.*

Adult silver dollars, Metynnis *spp., are good companions for larger South American and African riverine cichlids, but eat plants.*

Aquarists should refuse to buy cichlids such as these red parrot cichlids, "Cichlasoma" hybrid or mutation, that have been dyed various colors.

The male of this beautiful adult breeding pair of chocolate cichlids, Hypselecara temporalis, *is larger, more massively built, and has a higher rise to its forehead.*

(*Symphysodon aquifasciatus*) that prefer water in the mid-80s°F (29°C) be mixed with species that prefer it cooler.

✔ It is best if all the cichlids come from the same region of the world. Not only will they require similar water quality, but cichlids from different areas often have evolved very different behavioral "languages" that are not mutu-ally "understood." When two cichlid species that do not understand each other's "language" are placed together it often leads to severe fighting or outright killing.

✔ The fish should have differing territorial needs. For instance a bottom-dwelling cichlid can be combined with noncichlid species that prefer open water habitats. The need for

Do not buy congenitally deformed fish. In addition to having a notched back this angelfish also lacks ventral fins and has cataracts.

The popular rosy barb, **Puntius conchonius,** *is an active, hardy, and peaceful species that does well with small to medium-size, non-aggressive New and Old World cichlids.*

spawning territories should also be taken into consideration, and your aquarium should be set up in a manner that minimizes competition for spawning sites. Creative aquascaping can do much to develop separate territories within the confines of one aquarium (see the chapter on the cichlid aquarium, page 17).

✔ The fish should not look too much alike. Male cichlids of similar appearance tend to fight more than ones that look distinctly different.

✔ None of the species should be particularly aggressive. More information on this subject is given throughout this book and can be obtained in many of the other books listed in the Information section (page 92), from pet stores, and from fellow hobbyists.

Synodontis multipunctatus *is one of the many catfish of Lake Tanganyika.*

Rainbowfish come in a variety of sizes and are adaptable to the hard, alkaline conditions required by African Rift Lakes cichlids. This is a male Bleher's rainbowfish, **Cheilatherina bleheri.**

✔ The fish should all be of approximately the same size when introduced.

✔ The fish should have similar dietary needs. For example, plant and algae eaters, such as *Tropheus* spp. and the uaru, *Uaru amphia-canthoides*, require large amounts of bulk in their diets, and can develop fatal intestinal malfunctions if fed a low-fiber, primarily animal protein diet.

Dither and Target Fish

Noncichlids can also serve as *dither* or *target fish* in a cichlid aquarium. Dither fish is the term used to describe any outgoing, active, midwater species of fish that by its presence will help modify the behavior of shy, secretive, or nervous species of fish. Six or more schooling fish of the same species is preferable to one of six different species.

A target fish, on the other hand, is a fish most frequently added to an aquarium housing an adult pair of biparentally custodial (see Cichlid Reproduction, page 53) cichlids that have displayed considerable mutual aggression while attempting to develop a pair bond. The target fish is added to give these fish a target on which they can both vent their aggression, without harming each other. Needless to say, the tank must be large enough, and the target fish fast enough, for it to rapidly escape from the cichlids' aggressions.

Listed below are just a few of the fish that can, with careful selection of species, be compatible companions for cichlids.

Tetras and other characoid fish: Within this huge and diverse suborder of fish there are species that can provide companions for almost all but the most aggressive of non-African Rift Lakes cichlids. Most tetras are adaptable, hardy aquarium fish, doing well in water that is not overly hard, and slightly alkaline to moderately acidic in nature. Here are a few suggestions:

✔ The larger, nonpredacious African and South American tetras of the genera *Phenacogrammus* (Congo tetra), *Metynnis* (silver dollars), *Myleus* (red-hooks), *Triportheus* (elongate hatchetfish), *Chalceus*, and *Astyanax* are attractive companions for many kinds of reasonably peaceful, medium to large Central and South American cichlids such as the firemouth (*Thorichthys meeki*), eartheaters (*Satanoperca* and *Geophagus* spp.), severums (*Heros* spp.), festivums (*Mesonauta* spp.), chocolate cichlid (*Hypselacara temporalis*), and medium-size *Aequidens* types.

✔ On the other hand, if carefully selected, there are many brightly colored, smaller species of New World tetras, including neons and cardinal tetras (*Paracheirodon innesi* and *axelrodi*), the bloodfin (*Aphyocharax anisitsi*), and numerous species belonging to the genera *Hemigrammus* and *Hyphessobrycon*, that are perfect companions for the many West African and South American dwarf cichlids (genera *Pelvicachromis*, *Nanochromis*, *Apistogramma*, *Microgeophagus*, *Dichrossus*, and others).

Barbs: Barbs are Old World fish that, like tetras, come in a wide variety of sizes, many too large for the home aquarium. The black-spot barb (*Puntius filamentosus*), clown barb (*Barbodes everetti*), rosy barb (*P. conchonius*), arulius barb (*Capoeta arulius*), and other medium-size barbs are good companions for the same cichlids recommended as tankmates for the larger characins, whereas the smaller cherry barbs (*P. titteya*), checker barbs (*C. oligolepis*), and five-banded barb (*B. pentazona*) are suitable and colorful companions for West African and South American dwarf cichlids.

Rainbowfish: The rainbow fish of Australia, New Guinea, and Madagascar are perfect companions for many kinds of cichlids. Species vary in size from approximately 2 to 6 inches (5–15 cm). As a group they are easily fed and highly adaptable to a wide range of pH and water hardness. As a matter of fact, some of the Australian species, such as the various forms of the Australian rainbowfish, *Melanotaenia splendida*, can even adapt to the hard alkaline conditions required by African Rift lakes cichlids. The smaller Australian rainbows, such as McCulloch's Rainbowfish *(M. mccullochi)* are perfect dither fish for the frequently shy dwarf shell-dwelling cichlids from Lake Tanganyika. As an added bonus, rainbowfish prefer the upper reaches of the water column, thus providing activity to a portion of the aquarium normally shunned by cichlids.

Catfish: This huge suborder of fish can be found in temperate and tropical regions of both the Old and New Worlds. With so many species to choose from, there are catfish that can make interesting and suitable companions for a wide range of cichlids. Of particular interest are the suckermouth, algae-eating species belonging to the family Loricariidae. Not only does their armor-plated skin help provide protection from injury, but their appearance can almost be described as prehistoric. Their addiction to eating algae also provides a great service in keeping the aquarium attractive. The small *Otocinclus* and *Hypoptopoma* species are perfect additions to an aquarium housing most West African or South American dwarf cichlids, while the larger "plecostomus" and bristle-nose types (genus *Ancistrus*) do very well housed in large aquariums containing larger Central and South American cichlids. Bear in mind that these fish require hidden retreats in the form of rock shelters, or sections of PVC or clay pipe large enough for them to completely hide in. The ever-popular cory cats (*Corydoras* spp.) are small and attractive catfish that I have used successfully to serve as scavengers while at the same time adding variety to an aquarium housing peaceful dwarf cichlids, such as many of the genus *Apistogramma*. And finally, if your tastes run to the cichlids from Africa's Lakes Malawi and Tanganyika, the upside-down catfish of the genus *Synodontis* native to these lakes are an obvious choice.

THE CICHLID AQUARIUM

A "one size fits all" approach cannot be taken when it comes to setting up an aquarium for cichlids. Where your cichlids come from, their breeding biology, disposition, and behaviors will all affect the way you should set up their aquarium. Much of this will be discussed throughout this book. That being said, there are still many general considerations that the would-be cichlid aquarist should follow, and these will be discussed in this section.

Specifications

Shape

By choosing an aquarium with the greatest surface area without unduly sacrificing appearance you will be maximizing the ability for oxygen absorption and carbon dioxide purging at the water's surface. For most cichlids standard rectangular aquariums incorporate near ideal proportions; however, a proportionally longer, lower aquarium might be a better choice for bottom-dwelling, territorial species, or the sand-sifting geophagine eartheaters. On the other hand, if you are planning to keep the few high-bodied cichlid species, such as

The kribensis, Pelvicachromis pulcher (male shown), is one of many cichlids that will do well and readily spawn in a planted community aquarium.

angelfish and discus, the taller "show" models would be appropriate. Extremely tall, narrow aquariums should be avoided at all costs; they do not have enough surface or bottom area and their depth complicates cleaning and servicing.

Construction

The vast majority of aquariums sold today are of the so-called "all-glass" construction. These are frameless, and silicone cement is used to hold the panes together. The larger the aquarium, the thicker the glass. These aquariums are durable, attractive, and available in innumerable sizes and shapes

Aquariums of all sizes are also made of acrylic. The major advantages of an acrylic aquarium is that it is lighter in weight than an aquarium constructed of glass, and it is easier to drill and plumb for the installation of

CHECKLIST

Safety Precautions

A number of electrical appliances such as heaters, lights, and filters are required to run an aquarium. Whenever water is close to electricity there is the potential for danger. In order to avoid accidents you should observe the following safety rules:

1 All aquarium electrical devices should be UL-approved.

2 Electrical appliances operated within the aquarium must be specifically designed for submerged use.

3 Unplug all electric equipment before placing your hands in the aquarium.

4 For added safety, install an electronic safety device that will automatically shut off the current if any apparatus malfunctions.

5 Never attempt to do your own repairs on faulty equipment.

6 If any of the aquarium's electrical devices are plugged into an outlet below the water level of the aquarium, be certain to create a drip loop to prevent any water from trickling down the wire into the outlet, creating a short circuit.

specialized filter and water circulation systems. They also have less of a tendency to crack if subjected to accidental trauma. On the other hand, they are easily scratched and generally more expensive.

Note: Cichlids, especially during aggressive encounters, may attempt to jump out of the aquarium. Be sure to fit your aquarium with a tight-fitting cover.

Size

When selecting an aquarium always consider the size and behavior of the fish you intend to keep. Except for the Old and New World dwarf cichlids, most commonly kept cichlids are medium to large as far as aquarium fish go, and highly territorial. For these reasons I would consider a 50-gallon (190-L) aquarium as the smallest size to house a mixed group or an adult breeding pair of all but the smallest cichlids.

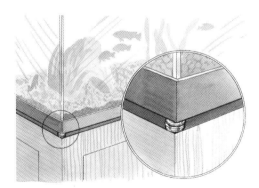

Make sure that your aquarium is situated on a stable, horizontal surface before filling it with water. If one corner is not evenly resting on the stand, place a penny or two under the part of the aquarium that is not firmly touching the stand.

Larger aquariums are also more forgiving of occasional errors in husbandry or equipment failures, and are more easily aquascaped in an attractive manner.

Location

Do not place your aquarium near a sunny window. Excessive sunlight will encourage the growth of unwanted algae, and could also cause your aquarium to overheat. For convenience, it is an asset to locate your aquarium near needed utilities such as water and electrical outlets.

Equipment

Heaters

Most cichlids require water temperatures between 75° and 81°F (24°–27°C), which can be properly maintained only with the help of a heater. There are many excellent thermostatically controlled heaters available at local pet stores. Some clip over the top edge of the aquarium while others are completely submersible. The advantage of the latter style is that there is less chance of accidentally having someone tamper with the setting. In selecting a heater of adequate size, a simple rule of thumb is to provide three watts of heat per gallon (3.8 L). A 50-gallon (190-L) aquarium would therefore require a 150-watt heater.

Thermometers

An aquarium thermometer is another essential piece of equipment. Unfortunately, many aquarium thermometers are very poorly made and highly inaccurate. It is therefore a good idea to check the thermometer against one that you know is accurate before you buy it.

TIP

Floors

If you plan to set up a large aquarium ask an architect or your landlord how much weight your floors are designed to support.

✔ One gallon (3.8 L) of water weighs 8.33 pounds (3.74 kg). A fully set-up 50-gallon (190-L) all-glass aquarium, complete with water, rocks, and gravel, will weigh at least 600 pounds (272 kg). The floors of many apartments and homes are not constructed to support such a massive, concentrated weight.

✔ People living in older buildings or upper floors should be particularly careful about checking the strength of their floors. In general, ground level or basement floors are usually of stronger construction than upper floors.

Air Pumps

An air pump is used to run air-driven filters (see page 22) and airstones. The vast majority of air pumps designed for the home aquarium are of the vibrator type, where a vibrating rubber diaphragm produces a flow of air. Well-made pumps of this style use very little electricity and are quite reliable. They are available in many sizes, producing differing amounts of air and head pressure. Before buying your pump discuss your needs with a knowledgeable pet store employee. Since the diaphragms of vibrator pumps fail with time, it is a good idea to obtain a repair kit complete

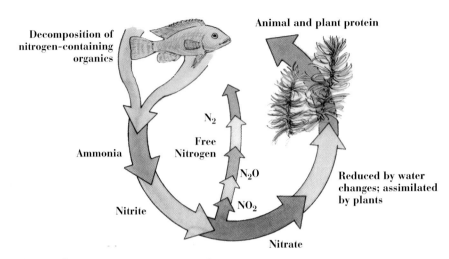

Animal and plant protein

Decomposition of
nitrogen-containing
organics

N_2

Free
Nitrogen

Ammonia

N_2O

Reduced by water
changes; assimilated
by plants

NO_2

Nitrite

Nitrate

The nitrification process in an aquarium.

with spare diaphragms when you buy your pump.

Note: An aquarium with proper filtration does not require additional airstones for aeration. The water circulation produced by the filter is more than adequate to ensure the proper levels of gas exchange at the water's surface. It is also unnecessary to purchase an air pump at all if your filters are motor driven, rather than run by a flow of air.

Filtration

The subject of filtration is complex; therefore, the information presented here should be thought of as a summary of the salient points to aid you in the selection of the proper filter system for your cichlid aquarium.

There are three major and distinctly different types of filtration: *mechanical, chemical,* and *biological.* Many aquarium filters simultaneously perform more than one of these processes.

Mechanical filtration: Simply put, mechanical filtration is the trapping of suspended particulate matter in the aquarium's water by passing it through a filtering medium, such as filter floss or a foam pad. With time, the filtering medium becomes clogged with debris and must be either washed or replaced.

Chemical filtration: In chemical filtration a chemically active substance is used to remove many nonammonia pollutants from the water, including medications, dyes, heavy metals, growth-inhibiting substances, and some proteins. The most commonly used chemical filtration medium is activated carbon. Other chemical filtration agents available to the home aquarist include ammonia-absorbing products, ion exchange resins, and phosphate-absorbing granules. With time, all of these eventually become deactivated and must be replaced.

Biological filtration: Without a doubt, this is the most important of the three types of aquarium filtration as far as the health of your aquarium's inhabitants are concerned. The breakdown of fish wastes and uneaten food produces organic compounds, several of which are highly toxic to fish. Primary among these is ammonia. In the two-step process of biological filtration, nitrifying bacteria first break down the ammonia into slightly less toxic nitrite, and finally into the relatively harmless nitrate ion. This process is known as *nitrification*. The beneficial bacteria responsble for this can grow on any substrate in the aquarium where they are exposed to oxygenated water. In a biological filter we maximize this effect by providing a volume of inert, porous material with a large surface area that these bacteria can colonize.

Note: The toxicity of ammonia (NH_3) is directly related to the aquarium water's pH (see pH, page 29). It is much more toxic under alkaline water conditions, which happens to be the required conditions for the successful maintenance of many cichlid species, particularly those from Africa's Rift Valley lakes. Under acidic conditions ammonia is present mainly in the much less toxic ammonium (NH_4+) ion.

Filter cycling: It takes approximately four to six weeks to grow a full compliment of nitrifying bacteria in a newly installed filter. Until this is accomplished there will not be enough bacteria present to adequately process the available fish wastes. The most common means of cycling a new aquarium is to add at first only a very few hardy, inexpensive, species of fish that are tolerant of high ammonia and

Taeniacara candidi is a South American dwarf cichlid that requires excellent biological filtration and soft, acidic water in order to thrive. (Male, lower fish.)

nitrite levels. Depending on the pH of your aquarium, some suggestions are mollies, gouramis, or even goldfish. These should be normally fed and cared for until the aquarium has fully cycled.

At first the ammonia levels will be seen to rise. This usually peaks in about a week and will then slowly drop as the population of ammonia-feeding bacteria develop. As the ammonia levels drop, that of nitrite will be seen to rise, but they too will soon start lowering as the nitrite-devouring bacteria increase in numbers. After the nitrite levels have returned to almost nondetectable levels you will find that the nitrate levels will start to rise, but much more slowly than you had observed with those of the ammonia and nitrite.

There are kits available for testing the levels of ammonia, nitrite, and nitrate in aquarium water. In a healthy, fully cycled aquarium the ammonia and nitrite levels should be close to zero. Nitrate levels should generally be kept below 80 ppm (for some delicate cichlid

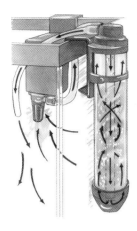
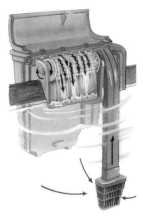

The fluidized bed filter (left) is one of the newest filters on the market; it provides excellent biological filtration. The Bio-wheel filter (right) is another excellent commercial filter. It provides all three types of filtration in an efficient arrangement.

species, such as discus and many species from the African Rift lakes, the nitrate level should be kept below 50 ppm). Although small amounts of the nitrate ion are utilized by aquarium plants as fertilizer, this is not nearly enough to prevent their buildup in the aquarium's water. The major method of eliminating nitrates is by performing periodic partial water changes (see Water Changes, page 33).

Filters

Remember, cichlids are voracious feeders and produce copious amounts of waste. Therefore, all but the most lightly stocked cichlid aquarium will require highly efficient filters large enough to adequately remove solid wastes and process all the dissolved nitrogenous compounds. Most filters will also require frequent cleaning to prevent their clogging with accumulated debris.

Air-Driven Filters

Sponge filters: Of simple construction and low cost, sponge filters are a very good choice for the small aquarium or quarantine tank, providing both mechanical and biological filtration. The pores of the sponge provide a great amount of surface area for bacteria to colonize and the constant flow of water through the sponge provides the bacteria with copious amounts of oxygenated water. Their main disadvantage is that they are difficult to disguise in an aesthetically decorated aquarium and, although they are available in a range of sizes, are still most suitable for aquariums under 20 gallons (76 L).

Hint: Well-established sponge filters can be effectively used in a newly set-up aquarium to "seed" it with the needed nitrifying bacteria.

Inside box filters: Also referred to as corner filters, these are basically small plastic boxes fitted with a perforated cover. They are quite inexpensive and come in a number of sizes and styles. The filtering materials of choice are placed in the box. The most common are a combination of a flosslike material and activated carbon. During operation water is drawn in through the perforations, passes over the filter media, and exits through the airlift tube. Although mainly a mechanical filter, they eventually develop biological activity as nitrifying bacteria become established within the filter media. When carbon or some other chemical filtration media is used, these filters also provide chemical filtration. Like the sponge filter, their main disadvantages are that they are hard to disguise and their generally small size limits them to use in small aquariums.

Hint: A box filter filled with activated carbon is a convenient way of removing medications from your aquarium's water after treatment is completed.

Undergravel filters: These are probably the most commonly employed filter system in home aquariums. When properly installed and serviced, undergravel filters can provide excellent mechanical and biological filtration, but they have some decided drawbacks, particularly when dealing with cichlids.

Their design consists of a perforated plastic plate that rests on the aquarium's bottom, and one or two associated lift tubes. A 2- to 3-inch (5–7.5-cm) layer of gravel is placed over the filter plate and serves as the filter medium. During operation water is drawn through the gravel and filter plate and exits via the lift tubes. Within limits, the greater the flow of water through the gravel, the greater the efficiency of the filter. There are special motor-driven water pumps, called powerheads, that fit on the tops of the lift tubes and greatly increase the filter's flow rate.

The major disadvantage of undergravel filters is that in heavily stocked aquariums they quickly become so clogged with debris that their efficiency is drastically decreased and they

Sponge filters provide excellent biological and mechanical filtration for a small aquarium without the risk of trapping tiny fry.

become little more than nitrate-producing factories, causing an associated drop in the aquarium's pH. Specially constructed gravel washers are available for vacuuming excess wastes from within the gravel bed, but their efficiency is limited. When dealing with cichlids, undergravel filters have another serious shortcoming: A large proportion of cichlids are prodigious and extensive diggers. This activity quickly exposes portions of the filter plate, thereby destroying its filtering action. There are ways to mitigate this, one being to lay down a layer of fiber screening over 1 or 2 inches (2.5–5 cm) of gravel and then adding another layer of gravel above that. Although this will prevent the cichlids from excavating clear down to the filter plate, it will also prevent you from performing the required gravel washing. In my opinion, the day of the undergravel filter has passed, and I recommend that you use a different type of filter for your cichlid aquarium.

Power Filters

Hang-on, or outside, power box filters: These filters conveniently hang from the aquarium's rim and utilize a motor to move water from the aquarium through the filtering media and back into the aquarium. The main

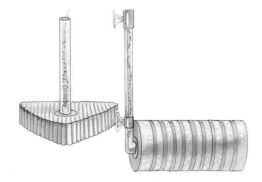

filter medium usually consists of floss, specially manufactured filter pads, or sponges, sometimes in combination with activated carbon. They come in numerous sizes and designs, and can provide excellent mechanical, biological, and chemical filtration for aquariums up to at least 100 gallons (380 L). For larger aquariums you can install two or more of these filters. Another advantage of this style filter is that the filter medium is easily observed to determine when it is dirty, and its replacement or cleaning is simple to perform.

Bio-wheel: A recent, excellent advance in the design of these filters is the incorporation of the so-called Bio-wheel, which significantly increases their biological filtering ability. In a Bio-wheel filter a partly submerged, rotating corrugated wheel is located in the pathway of the water's return to the aquarium. The wheel's large surface area, combined with its exposure to an abundance of oxygen, permits large

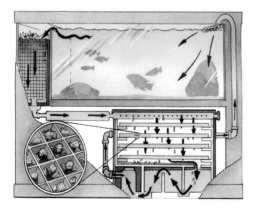

The trickle filter provides excellent biological filtration. A prefilter in the overflow box or within the filter serves as a mechanical filter.

numbers of nitrifying bacteria to colonize its surface. I highly recommend these filters for use in a cichlid aquarium.

Canister Filters

Canister filters are generally large, high-output filters. A motor pulls the water through a length of flexible tubing from the aquarium into the canister, through the filtering media, and pumps it back into the aquarium via another section of hose. Most permit the aquarist to install a variety of filter materials, ranging from sponges, gravel of various sizes, biological filtering media, and activated carbon pillows. Their efficiency and large capacity permit them to be used on larger aquariums. Their disadvantages are that in a heavily stocked aquarium they quickly clog with detritus resulting in a dramatic decrease in flow rate of water through them. They are also rather expensive, and difficult and messy to clean. These filters run under pressure, necessitating that all fittings be tightly secured if costly leaks or floods are to be avoided.

Trickle Filters

Sometimes referred to as wet-dry filters, a trickle filter is one of the most efficient biological filters available for a large home aquarium. After passing through a pre-filter that removes all large particulates, the water trickles through a chamber housing an inert, nonpacking filtering medium. Here, the abundance of oxygen permits enormous numbers of nitrifying bacteria to thrive on the medium's surface. The water then enters a sump before being returned to the aquarium by a water pump. Because of their efficiency, trickle filters are popular for aquariums that are heavily stocked or house fish that demand excellent water quality (many aquarists consider them the filter of choice for marine and reef-type aquariums where water quality is paramount). Formerly, the installation of a trickle filter required that the aquarium be drilled and plumbed. This is no longer the case as there are now many models that hang from the aquarium's upper rim. Disadvantages of trickle filters are that they are rather pricey, and their large water pumps tend to increase the aquarium's temperature. In addition, they are somewhat bulky, usually being installed below or behind the aquarium.

Fluidized Bed Filters

Long used by public aquariums, smaller models are now available to the home aquarist. Aquarium water is pumped *upward* through a chamber filled with an insoluble sand. The water then returns to the aquarium through some sort of an overflow system. A pre-filter on the pump blocks the entry of particulate matter into the filter chamber. Because the power of the upwardly flowing water keeps the sand in a semisuspended state, nitrifying bacteria are able to colonize all the surfaces of each grain of sand. Although small in size, they provide just about the best biological filtration imaginable. Their main disadvantage is that fluidized bed filters (see page 22) are *not* mechanical or chemical filters, and a separate mechanical filter must also be used.

Lighting

Cichlids come from waters with vastly different light conditions, but if extremes are avoided, hardly any of them seem demanding in this respect. The main objectives should be

This large male frontosa, Cyphotilapia frontosa, *from Lake Tanganyika, has selected a clay pipe as its shelter.*

to provide enough light to satisfactorily view the fish, and if you have live plants, to provide lighting of suitable intensity and wavelengths to ensure their robust growth.

Fluorescent Lights

Fluorescent lights are the best and most economical means of lighting the average cichlid aquarium. Most commercial aquarium hoods are designed for this type of lighting. Fluorescent lights are available in a number of different spectrums. For most freshwater aquariums, including those for cichlids, I recommend using the "daylight" tubes, as these provide the most natural appearance. Tubes that produce a lot of red light, such as "plant-gro" tubes, should be avoided since they distort the colors of the fish and encourage unwanted algae growth. The light output of fluorescent tubes deteriorates with time, and they should be replaced on an average of every 12 months in an unplanted aquarium, or more frequently when live plants are present. If you are using a multitube fixture change one tube at a time in rotation to minimize fluctuations in light intensity.

If you require more light than the average aquarium fixture produces, it is worth looking into the more specialized lighting systems that utilize HO (high output) or VHO (very high output) types of fluorescent lights. These are particularly useful in planted or unusually deep aquariums.

Metal Halide Lighting

Metal halide lighting is another possibility where intense lighting is required. Disadvantages are their relatively high price and the great amount of heat that they produce.

Substrate

What and how much substrate is to be used in a cichlid aquarium is influenced by whether or not you intend to grow aquatic plants or use an undergravel filter, and the type of cichlids you wish to keep. Both an undergravel filter and live rooted plants will require a gravel depth of at least 1½ to 2½ inches (3.8–6.4 cm). If neither of these is of concern, you need use only enough gravel to cover the aquarium's bottom.

River Gravel

River gravel with a diameter of ⅛ to ⅜ of an inch (3–8 mm) makes an excellent substrate for the vast majority of cichlid aquariums. Unless your tap water is extremely soft and you are keeping cichlids that require alkaline water conditions, limestone gravels should be avoided.

Local pet stores stock a wide variety of aquarium gravel in many colors, including natural. Most fish look their best against a substrate of natural, dark brown, or black gravel. Avoid crushed lava gravel as the particles are extremely rough and sharp and can damage a cichlid's mouth. For aquariums being set up to house cichlids from Africa's Rift Valley lakes a calcium-rich substrate, such as crushed dolomitic limestone, is useful in maintaining the hard and alkaline conditions these fish prefer.

Note: No matter what type of gravel you use, always wash it thoroughly before placing it in the aquarium.

Decorative Materials

Rocks

Rocks, or other material that can provide shelter and spawning sites, are essential for most cichlid species. Rocks may be arranged to form piles, caves, grottos, or isolated groupings, the actual arrangement depending to a large degree upon the natural environment and habits of the cichlids you intend to keep. For instance, open-substrate spawners (see Cichlid Reproduction, page 53) do not require the grottolike structures required by cave spawners, while for rock-dwelling mbuna cichlids (see page 78) of Lake Malawi you might wish to cover the rear half of the aquarium clear up to the surface with carefully stacked and piled rocks.

Not all rocks are suitable for aquarium use, as some may contain harmful chemicals. In general, rocks too hard to be easily scratched with the blade of a penknife are safe.

Avoid sharp, rough-surfaced rocks such as lava and coral skeletons in a freshwater aquarium. Most pet stores stock a wide variety of aquarium rocks, and I advise you to speak with an employee about their selection and arrangement.

Bogwood

Bogwood is also very useful for furnishing your aquarium, and can help create naturalistic environments for many Congo and South American cichlids. You can collect your own from nearby, unpolluted bogs or buy it from pet stores. Bogwood that has been permitted to dry out will generally be buoyant and float when placed in your aquarium. To rectify this situation it can either be screwed to a piece of slate heavy enough to keep it on the bottom, or with the aid of a heavy rock kept totally submerged in a pail of water until it becomes totally waterlogged.

Caution: Bogwood may contain tannins and humic acids that can lower an aquarium's pH, and must be thoroughly leached before being used in aquariums housing cichlids coming from alkaline waters.

Artificial Shelters

Where aesthetics is not the primary concern, objects such as flowerpots laid on their side and sections of PVC pipe are popular cichlid aquarium furnishings. They may not be pretty to look at, but they are easily cleaned, inexpensive, and are readily accepted by the fish as shelters and breeding sites.

Plants

Live plants are not suitable for all cichlid tanks. Many species of cichlids, such as the uaru (*Uaru amphiacanthoides*) and mbuna

TIP

Rocks and Their Foundation

Rocks and other heavy objects used within the aquarium must rest on a solid foundation, such as the aquarium bottom, and not just placed on top of the gravel. If this is not done, the prodigious digging activities of the cichlids will quickly lead to the undermining and collapse of the rock structures. Toppling rocks have more than once been the cause of a cracked aquarium glass.

species are confirmed plant eaters, and will make short work of any living plants. Many larger cichlids from South America and Africa may not actually eat plants, but their constant digging and rearrangement of the gravel will quickly uproot them (this can be partially mitigated by placing small stones around the plants' bases, or planting them in small containers). Yet, where suitable, plants can provide great beauty in a cichlid aquarium.

In general, select plants with tough, broad leaves. Amazon sword plants (*Echinodorus* spp.), cryptocorynes, *Anubias* spp., Java fern (*Microsorium pteropus*), and the various *Sagittaria* species are all good choices. Java fern should not be rooted in the gravel, but tied to a piece of bogwood, or a rock with an irregular surface. In a short period of time its roots will become firmly attached to these substrates and it will grow into a glorious clump of dark green leaves. Floating plants such as water fern (*Ceratopterus cornuta*), hornwort

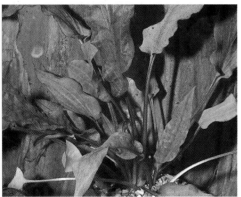

Top left: A healthy Amazon swordplant,
Echinodorus *spp., is a perfect centerpiece*
for a large aquarium.

Bottom left: Many of the "Crypts," including
this **Cryptocoryne wendtii,** *are durable*
and adaptable aquarium plants with very
tough leaves.

Top right: The Java fern, **Microsorum**
pteropus, *is one of the easiest-grown*
aquarium plants. An added plus is that
it is ignored by many plant-eating
cichlids.

Bottom right: **Anubias barteri** *is known for*
its toughness and ease of cultivation.

(*Ceratophyllum* spp.), and duckweed (*lemna* spp.) also have their place in some cichlid aquariums either as food items or to provide security and shade.

In aquariums with inadequate light for live plants or where there are plant-destroying fish present the use of plastic plants is an option. Many are very well made and realistic in appearance.

The Water

One of the most important requirements for keeping fish healthy is that their water be of the proper quality. This includes, but is not limited to, low levels of dissolved organics such as ammonia, nitrite, and nitrates (see Filtration, page 20), and proper pH and water hardness.

pH

pH is the standard unit for measuring the acidity or alkalinity of aquarium water, and stands for "potential of hydrogen." A pH of 7.0 is considered neutral. Readings below 7.0 are considered acidic, while those above 7.0 are alkaline.

Water Hardness

Water hardness is a measurement of the amount of certain ions dissolved in water, most notably calcium and magnesium. There are various ways of measuring this including carbonate hardness, total hardness, and electrical conductivity (the harder the water, the greater the conductivity). To further confuse things there are also a number of scales used to express hardness. The two most common are milligrams per liter (mg/L), which is virtually equivalent to parts per million (ppm), and degrees of German hardness (°dH). One °dH

Water Hardness

mg/L CaCo$_3$	°dH	Considered
0–50	0–3	soft
51–100	3–6	moderately soft
101–200	6–12	slightly hard
201–300	12–18	moderately hard
301–450	18–25	hard

equals 17.9 ppm. Conductivity is measured in microseimens, a reading that can be converted to an approximate equivalent in ppm.

Pet stores sell many different brands of test kits and meters for measuring pH and hardness. Most sold in America measure hardness in ppm calcium carbonate (CaCo$_3$) hardness.

Many cichlids are highly adaptable, thriving in average tap water conditions (pH 6.5–7.5; 50–200 ppm carbonate hardness), but it is still best to attempt duplicating the water quality found in their natural environment. For delicate species and for breeding of many cichlids attention to pH and hardness is essential. Most South American cichlids from the Amazon and Orinoco River basins prefer water that is slightly acidic to neutral and moderately soft. This is very different from the hard and alkaline conditions preferred—or required—by cichlids from Africa's Rift Valley lakes.

Reverse osmosis unit: Hard water can be softened by diluting it with a portion of clean rain- or distilled water. If you will require large amounts of soft water you might consider buying a reverse osmosis unit. These units come in different sizes and filter out dissolved minerals from tap water, but they are quite wasteful—usually about 5 to 7 gallons (19–26 L) of water is wasted for each gallon (3.8 L) of demineralized water produced. Soft water can be made harder by using a limestone gravel as a substrate or in the filter, or by the addition of commercial products available at pet stores. There are also numerous products available for changing and stabilizing an aquarium's pH.

Note: Soft water has much less buffering capacity than hard water, and it takes careful husbandry and regular monitoring to avoid a disastrous drop in pH.

As we have seen, the cichlid family is exceedingly diverse, with species coming from a wide variety of environments and geographic regions. A properly set-up aquarium is pleasing to look at and satisfies the needs of the cichlid species it contains. In order to accomplish these goals you, as an aquarist, must develop both a sense of aesthetics as well as an in-depth knowledge of cichlids.

Refer to text for detailed instructions.

Step 3. Add gravel and, if desired, an undergravel filter.

Steps 4 and 5. After adding rocks and bogwood, fill aquarium about halfway with water. Live or plastic plants can then be added.

Duplicating a Natural Environment

As far as aquarium fish health is concerned, the best results are obtained when an attempt is made to duplicate the natural environment of a particular cichlid species, both in regards to aquascaping and water quality. Although some cichlids are much more adaptable than others, this should not be used as an excuse for maintaining them in unsuitable aquarium conditions. The needs of your fish should always be the paramount consideration. These needs will significantly influence such basic essentials as the size of your aquarium, the type, amount, and arrangement of rock work, the presence or absence of plants, and the grain size and type of gravel you should use.

Step-by-Step Set Up

That being said, the actual steps involved in setting up an aquarium are quite constant no matter how the end result will look.

1. Select an appropriate location for your aquarium, taking great care that it is completely level.

2. Wash the aquarium thoroughly with lukewarm

FISH TANK

water, using a new plastic pot scrubber to clean all inside surfaces of debris and stains. Do not use any sort of soap or cleanser as they might leave a toxic residue. If your aquarium is of acrylic construction be certain that you use a scrubber pad specifically made to clean plastic without causing scratches.

3. Thoroughly wash the gravel that will be used as the substrate. This should be done in a container other than the aquarium. Be certain to continue rinsing the gravel until the waste water runs clear. The amount of gravel and its type will depend on such variables as the type of filter to be used, whether or not you will be using live plants, and the varieties of cichlids that will inhabit the completed aquarium (see Substrate, page 26). After the gravel has been washed it should be carefully added to the aquarium.

Note: If you are going to use an undergravel filter, it should be placed in the aquarium before adding the gravel.

4. Fill the aquarium about halfway with water of the proper temperature. You can direct the flow of water over a flat rock or saucer to keep it from stirring up the gravel.

5. Now is the time to add any rocks, bogwood, and other furnishings. To prevent the rocks from shifting, or being undermined by the digging action of the cichlids, be certain that they are resting solidly on the aquarium's bottom or undergravel filter plate. This is very important in preventing a rock from toppling and cracking a glass wall of the aquarium. After you are pleased with the placement of these furnishings you should then add any live or plastic plants.

6. Complete the filling of the aquarium and add all technical equipment such as the heater,

Steps 6 and 7. Completely fill aquarium and add all mechanical equipment.

thermometer, and filters (unless you are using an undergravel filter that had been added earlier). This is also the time to add any water conditioner such as a chloramine neutralizer.

7. Put the light and hood in place, turn on all equipment to see that everything is running properly, and set your heater to the proper temperature. After your aquarium has reached the correct temperature you may "inoculate" the aquarium with nitrifying bacteria by adding a handful of gravel, or some used filter material from a well-established, healthy aquarium. This will significantly shorten the time it takes for the aquarium to fully cycle.

8. Wait at least 3 to 4 days to make certain that everything is running well before adding any fish. To prevent overloading the limited biological filtering activity of a newly set-up aquarium, the fish should be added a few at a time over a period of weeks. You should always check that the ammonia and nitrite levels are within safe limits before adding more (see Filter Cycling, page 21).

AQUARIUM CARE AND MAINTENANCE

Regular aquarium maintenance helps to create an optimum environment for your cichlids. Although it does not involve much time, routine maintenance should not be overlooked or ignored.

You should check daily all aquarium equipment to make certain it is running properly, examine all fish for signs of disease, and remove all uneaten food—there should be none if they are being fed properly. The cleaning or changing of filter media, trimming of dead and decayed leaves from plants, and the removal of algae from the glass should be performed as needed. There are special magnetic algae removal pads sold at pet stores that make this last chore a simple matter.

Water Changes

One of the most important and frequently overlooked aspects of aquarium husbandry is regular partial water changes. Cichlids are voracious feeders and produce copious amounts of liquid and solid wastes. Regardless

Proper care of Rift Lakes cichlids, such as this yellow peacock, **Aulonocara baenschi,** *requires regular water testing and aquarium maintenance.*

of the efficiency of your filter system, unless your aquarium is very lightly stocked, this quickly results in high levels of dissolved proteinacious compounds and nitrates that will adversely affect the health of your fish.

The average cichlid aquarium will require a 10–20 percent water change weekly; in the case of large cichlids or a very heavily stocked tank a 30–40 percent weekly water change is not excessive. Notable exceptions are the cichlids from Lake Tanganyika that resent large-volume water changes. On the other hand, a moderate-size aquarium housing only one breeding pair or trio of a dwarf cichlid, or a larger one with a single breeding pair of discus or angels might do well with a 10–15 percent change every two weeks.

How you go about performing the water change depends primarily on the size and number of aquariums you have. A length of siphon hose and a 5-gallon (19-L) bucket is satisfactory for changing the water of one small aquarium. With larger or more tanks a siphon hose long enough to reach from your

Treating New Water
Always make certain that the new water is treated with a product that destroys chlorine and chloramines and is the same temperature, pH, and hardness as that in the aquarium.

aquarium to a sink or other drain is the best option. At most pet stores you can buy clear plastic siphon hoses up to 20 feet (6 m) long that have a faucet adapter attached to one end. With these it is a simple matter to connect the hose directly to a faucet for refilling your aquarium.

Gravel Cleaning

In aquariums with only a thin layer of gravel, regular siphoning of accumulated waste from the gravel's surface is all that is needed. This is different from the gravel cleaning required in aquariums with a thick layer of gravel, or ones with undergravel filters. This is easily accomplished with a product called a *gravel washer*, which is simply a siphon equipped with a section of rigid plastic tube that is about three to four times greater in diameter than the siphon hose. The wide end is placed into the gravel and the siphon started. Because of its wide diameter, the detritus is sucked through the siphon, but the heavier gravel is left behind. Gravel washing should be avoided near plants in order to avoid damaging their roots.

Filter Cleaning

Filters should be regularly checked to ensure that the filter media is not becoming clogged with accumulated debris. How often this will occur depends on the number and size of the fish in the aquarium and the size of the filter. Do not clean your filters more frequently than is needed since cleaning eliminates the beneficial nitrifying bacteria inhabiting the filter media, thereby destroying much of its ability to perform biological filtration. To keep motor-driven filters working properly, each time the filter is serviced the impeller assembly should be cleaned of accumulated slime and detritus buildup. For the technique of cleaning undergravel filters, see the previous section on gravel washing.

Hint: To minimize the destruction of a filter's biological activity, replace or wash only a portion of the filter media at each cleaning.

Nutrition

Cichlids as a group have evolved to utilize virtually all available aquatic food sources. Although most are generalized predators, others feed on other fish, microplankton, insects, aquatic plants, scales of other fish, or aufwuchs (a term describing the combination of algae and microorganisms that live on submerged rocks and wood). Fortunately for the aquarist, most cichlids are highly adaptable when it comes to their food, greedily consuming most commercially available dry, frozen, and live foods of appropriate sizes.

Note: The digestive system of some specialized plant- and algae-eating cichlids is especially adapted to these high-roughage foods. Feeding them a low-roughage, meat-based diet will result in severe digestive disturbances and is one of the purported causes of the deadly condition known as Malawi bloat (see Diseases and Treatments, page 41).

Dry Foods

Dry foods are available as flakes and both sinking and floating forms of pellets, sticks, and granules. Whereas the flake form is perfectly suitable for small cichlids, the larger pellets and sticks are more appropriate for larger fish. For most cichlids these foods can serve as their staple diet. Reputable brands are well formulated, and fortified with vitamins, minerals, and natural color enhancers. They are also available in many different formulations to satisfy the dietary requirements of carnivorous, omnivorous, and vegetarian cichlid species.

Frozen and Fresh Foods

Even though most of the commonly kept cichlids will do well on a diet composed exclusively of dry foods, they all do better with regular additions of frozen, fresh, and live foods. This becomes particularly important when conditioning your cichlids for breeding and raising small fry, or in the maintenance of the more delicate species. Some frozen fish foods relished by cichlids are brine shrimp, daphnia, mosquito larvae, bloodworms (larvae of chironomid midge insects, often erroneously sold as "red mosquito larvae"), and both the large and small species of the marine crustaceans commonly called krill (*Euphasia* spp.). Other well-accepted foods are minced shrimp, clams,

A gravel washer is a great aid in cleaning accumulated detritus from your aquarium's gravel.

and other seafoods, as well as whole or chopped frozen minnows. Which of these are the right choices for your cichlids has a lot to do with their size and dietary requirements. It should be noted that there are some excellent frozen food mixtures available at pet stores. Some of these have gelatin added as a binder. Read their ingredient list carefully, as some are much better than others.

Beef heart: Two foods that have elicited great debate within the hobby are beef heart and tubifex worms. Although beef heart is an excellent protein source, it is lacking in a number of essential vitamins and minerals. Because it is low in roughage, it has long been targeted

Beef heart has been implicated as a major cause of severe digestive disturbances in Tropheus duboisi *and others of its genus. These highly vegetarian cichlids should be fed several small meals daily that contain adequate vegetable matter.*

The smaller algae-eating catfish of the family Loricariidae, such as this unidentified Panaque *from the Peruvian Amazon, make excellent additions to an aquarium with suitable cichlids. They will also reduce the need for the aquarist to clean unwanted algae from the aquarium glass.*

Placing the generic name of the green terror, "Aequidens" rivulatus, in quotes indicates that its taxonomic status is uncertain.

Above: Discus fish (Symphysodon aequifasciatus) *are disc-shaped and laterally compressed.*

Above right: Regan's dwarf pike cichlid, Crenicichla regani, *is a torpedo-shaped predator. A male of this widespread species is shown. Females display one to three conspicuous black eye-spots on the dorsal fin.*

The false basket-mouth, Acaronia nassa, *has a more "typical" fish shape.*

CHECKLIST

Hints for Feeding Cichlids

1 Feed a varied diet. This helps prevent nutritional deficiencies.

2 Feed most adult cichlids twice daily. Exceptions are algae or plankton grazers that should be fed small portions more frequently, and fish predators that are usually fed large food items less frequently.

3 Feed cichlid fry at least three times daily. Feeding less can result in stunted growth.

4 Feed only as much as will be totally consumed in three to five minutes

5 The bigger the cichlid, the larger the food morsel that should be offered.

as a cause of digestive disturbances in many African cichlids. For this reason it should be fed in very small amounts, if at all, to specialized zooplankton pickers and aufwuchs feeders, such as many of the haplochromines and the genus *Tropheus*. If you choose to feed beef heart to your cichlids, be certain to first trim it of all indigestible fat and fibrous tissue, and make certain that it does not comprise more than 20 percent of their diet.

Tubifex: Tubifex is a totally different matter. These small worms inhabit some of the most polluted aquatic environments imaginable, and no matter how well they are washed, it is impossible to totally purge them of potential pathogens. The sad tales of aquarists having lost valuable fish to systemic bacterial infections after being fed tubifex are legion. Although fish love them, I recommend that they never be used as fish food, whether they are live, frozen, or freeze-dried.

Vegetable matter: Many cichlids appreciate supplementary feedings of fresh vegetable matter. Some suggestions along these lines are duckweed and other tender aquatic plants, cooked peas and lima beans, romaine lettuce, spinach, and zucchini. The last two should be blanched or steamed before being offered.

Live Food

Many of the recommended frozen foods can be bought or collected in the live form. These include minnows and other "feeder" fish, mosquito larvae, daphnia, and adult brine shrimp. There are also live foods that can be cultured at home. Some of the best are feeder guppies, earthworms, white worms, Grindel worms, and baby brine shrimp. White worm and Grindel worm cultures, complete with instructions, are available from specialty dealers listed in aquarium magazine classified sections. They are excellent foods for small or baby cichlids, while earthworms, fed either chopped or whole, are greedily consumed by larger cichlids. Brine shrimp eggs (cysts) are sold at most pet stores and are easily hatched at home in a saltwater solution (see page 62). Newly hatched brine shrimp are an essential and nourishing first food for most baby cichlids, and can even be raised at home to adulthood.

Many hobbyists believe that some cichlids, such as Oscars and pike cichlids (*Crenicichla* spp.), will accept only live fish as food. Not only is this an erroneous assumption, but a diet comprised exclusively of one type of feeder fish can result in dietary deficiencies. It is best to condition these species to accept other foods, including chopped minnows, chunk fish and seafood flesh, frozen large krill (*Euphasia superba*), earthworms, and even pellet and stick dry foods. It may take some patience, but it can be done.

Note: Live fish used as food can be a source of serious diseases and parasites. They should always be quarantined for at least two weeks and fed only when you are reasonably certain that they are disease free. This is one of the reasons that I recommend using previously frozen feeders, as the freezing process kills many pathogenic organisms.

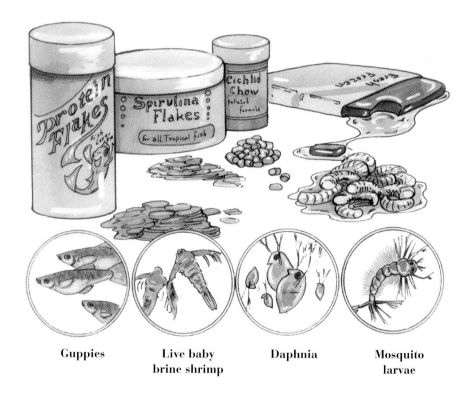

| Guppies | Live baby brine shrimp | Daphnia | Mosquito larvae |

A varied diet is important for the overall well-being of your cichlids.

DISEASES AND TREATMENTS

When it comes to fish diseases, an ounce of prevention is worth a pound of cure.

The Quarantine Tank

A quarantine period of three to four weeks for all newly purchased cichlids is the best way of preventing the introduction of diseases into your aquarium. Even if at the time of purchase a fish shows no outward signs of disease or parasites, it could be carrying them in a latent or subclinical form. The quarantine aquarium need only be large enough to house your average new purchases. It should be furnished with a cover, heater, small inside box or sponge filter, and some rocks or clean clay flowerpots to serve as hiding places. All fish in quarantine should be carefully examined at least twice daily and treated immediately and appropriately if any health problems are noted.

Other methods of preventing diseases are to feed a balanced diet, provide your cichlids with their preferred water quality and aquarium furnishing, and avoid keeping incompatible species together. Stress significantly reduces

Early head and lateral line erosion in a green discus, **Symphysodon aequifasciatus** *(see page 46).*

the immune system of fish, making them more susceptible to disease.

Some Common Cichlid Diseases

The following pages discuss some of the diseases that most frequently affect cichlids. Of course, there are many others that may occasionally be seen. Fortunately for the aquarist, most of the more common diseases have distinctive, easily recognized symptoms.

Important Note: Activated carbon will remove most medications from the water, and it should be removed from your filter before beginning treatment. When treatment is completed, fresh carbon can be used to remove leftover medication from the water.

Ich, or White Spot Disease

Symptoms: Small white dots resembling small grains of salt that gradually increase in number appear on the fish's body, fins, and gills. Fish with this disease frequently scratch themselves against objects in the aquarium in a futile attempt to rid themselves of these irritating parasites. Highly contagious.

Cause: The ciliated protozoan *Ichthyophthirius multifilis*. Only a portion of this parasite's life cycle is spent on a fish. When the organism matures it leaves its host, settles to the bottom, and forms a cyst-like structure. Within this capsule it repeatedly divides until there may be thousands of daughter cells. The cyst then bursts and the immature parasites swim through the water seeking a host fish, then crawl around awhile over the fish before penetrating the skin's surface layer and growing to maturity.

Treatment: The ich parasite is only susceptible to treatment in the free-swimming and crawler stage. There are many proprietary formulations for treating ich available at pet stores. The most effective of these contain malachite green by itself or in combination with formalin. Follow the manufacturer's directions carefully, and treat until at least three days after the last white dots disappear—usually seven to ten days at normal aquarium temperature.

Ich is the most common of all aquarium fish diseases. Fortunately it is has easily noticed, distinctive symptoms and is just as easily treated if caught early.

Slimy Skin, or Blue Slime Disease

Symptoms: Overproduction of mucus by the fish, resulting in a bluish, slimy haze that gradually increases in area to eventually cover the fish's body and fins. It frequently begins on the back near the dorsal fin. Affected fish are sluggish, show labored breathing, and refuse food. Progress of this disease can be slow to rapid depending on the causative agent. Once the gills are affected the fish will rapidly die from suffocation. Highly contagious.

Cause: Several ciliated or flagellated parasitic protozoa belonging to the genera *Ichthyobodo* (formerly *Costia*), *Chilodonella, Trichodina,* and others that can only be accurately identified under a microscope. Knowing the actual causative agent is unimportant as treatment is the same for all.

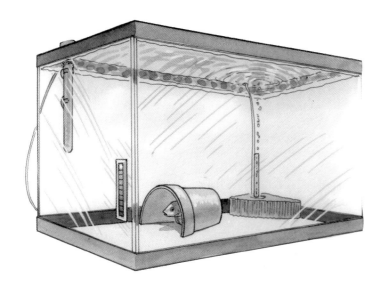

A quarantine and/or hospital aquarium should be a simple setup with a filter, heater, and hiding place. In this type of aquarium, it is easier to observe the fish for any signs of change in its condition.

Treatment: There are many commercially available products for the treatment of this disease, my favorite being two drops of concentrated (37 percent) formalin added to each gallon (3.8 L) of aquarium water every three days for a total of three treatments. When using formalin, always make certain that the aquarium is well aerated.

Body Fungus, or Cotton Wool Disease

Symptoms: One or more tufts of whitish growth resembling small tufts of cotton or bread mold appearing anywhere on a fish's fins or body. This disease invariably appears as a secondary invader of damaged tissue. Once established, it will spread rapidly to healthy tissue. This disease is frequently encountered in cichlids because their aggressiveness often results in lost scales, wounds, and torn fins. Not contagious in the usual sense.

Cause: Fungi of the genus *Saprolegnia* and related genera. These are the same fungi that grow on uneaten food, dead fish, and infertile eggs.

Treatment: This disease must be caught early for treatment to be successful. If only one or two fish are affected, it is best to remove them to a hospital aquarium for treatment. One tablespoon of rock salt per gallon (3.8 L) of water is often effective, although a few cichlids that come from very soft water may be sensitive to this high a concentration of salt. This much salt will kill plants and snails. There are also numerous antifungal medications available at pet stores. Use according to the manufacturer's directions. In stubborn cases the drug Griseofulvin used as a long-term bath at a concentration of 38 mg per gallon (10 mg per L) has been recommended.

This prescription drug must be obtained from a veterinarian.

Note: To prevent repeated outbreaks of this disease, remove any overly aggressive fish from your aquarium and increase the number of hiding places.

Bacterial Fin Rot

Symptoms: Rapidly progressive fraying and disintegration of the fins and tail, until only inflamed stubs remain. It often appears secondary to injury. Moderately contagious.

Cause: Gram-negative bacteria, mainly of the genus *Flexibacter*.

Treament: Broad-spectrum antibiotics that are effective against gram-negative bacteria, including tetracyclines and the nitrofurazones. The disease frequently does not respond well to treatment due to the numerous antibiotic-resistant strains of the causative bacteria.

Hexamitosis

Symptoms: This disease commonly affects cichlids. Some species, such as discus and angelfish, appear particularly susceptible. The classic symptom is slimy, whitish feces that appear as if the fish is excreting its intestinal lining. Secondary symptoms are loss of appetite, darkening or fading of normal coloration, and a tendency to remain inactive and in hiding. Contagious.

Cause: Intestinal flagellated protozoa of the genera *Hexamita* (synonym *Octomitus*) and *Spironucleus*. Their presence irritates the intestinal lining, resulting in the secretion of excess mucus by the intestine. Heavy parasite loads can lead to peritonitis, and spread of the parasites to other internal organs. The progress of the disease is not usually rapid, but left untreated it is fatal.

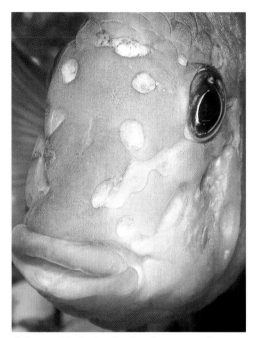

Advanced hole-in-the-head on a pearl eartheater, Geophagus brasiliensis.

The fins of this angelfish have been mostly destroyed by bacterial fin rot.

This Oscar has a severe case of ich.

The white cottonlike growth on the tail of this taillight shiner (not a cichlid) is caused by the fungus Saprolegnia.

The injuries to this bumblebee cichlid, Metriaclima crabro, are the result of aggression.

The distended abdomen of this female peacock cichlid (Aulonocara sp.), *is the classic sign of Malawi bloat.*

The uaru, uaru amphiacanthoides, *is a delicate species requiring careful management.*

The firemouth cichlid, thorichthys meeki, *is a hardy species that rarely becomes ill.*

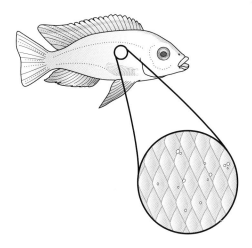

Ich is a common disease of all aquarium fish. (See photo, page 41.)

Treatment: Any proprietary fish medication containing the drug metronidazole (Flagyl). Follow the manufacturer's directions carefully.

Malawi Bloat

Symptoms: This condition mainly affects planktivorous and aufwuchs-feeding cichlids from Lakes Tanganyika and Malawi. The primary symptom is an increasing distension of the abdominal area, giving the fish the appearance of having eaten too much. This is usually accompanied by rapid respiration, lethargy, and a loss of appetite. Death occurs within a very few days.

Note: It is easy to confuse this illness with dropsy, a condition caused by fluid retention secondary to kidney failure. In dropsy, unlike Malawi bloat, the scales become raised, giving the fish the appearance of a pinecone. There is no cure for dropsy, and affected fish should be euthanized. (See photo, page 45.)

Cause: The abdominal distension is caused by general inflammation and swelling of the intestinal tract and associated organs. The exact cause of this condition is still a matter of debate. It is generally agreed that a diet high in animal protein such as beef heart, and low in roughage, possibly complicated by intestinal parasites such as *Hexamita* and nematode worms, are predisposing factors. Overfeeding has also been implicated. Frequently a number of fish within an aquarium may come down with this disease, but it is not known if this is evidence of contagion or poor husbandry.

Treatment: Some authorities recommend treating the entire aquarium with Metronidazole to eliminate intestinal protozoa, plus a broad-spectrum antibiotic that is readily absorbed into the fish, such as nitrofurazone. Unfortunately, treatment is often unsuccessful. It is easier to prevent this illness by feeding susceptible species a diet high in vegetable matter and roughage, and offering all foods in small amounts several times a day, rather than in one or two large feedings.

Hole-in-the-Head, or Head and Lateral Line Erosion (HLLE)

Symptoms: This highly disfiguring malady begins as a series of small pits, usually near the eyes. Left unchecked, it develops into extensive, cavitating, noninflamed erosions of the head. Advanced cases may involve the region of the lateral line, and fin edges. Amazingly, even fish with advanced HLLE feed and act normally, and do not appear to be in discomfort. (See photos, pages 40 and 44.)

Good husbandry practices help prevent bloat (top) and hole-in-the-head disease (bottom). (See photos, pages 44 and 45.)

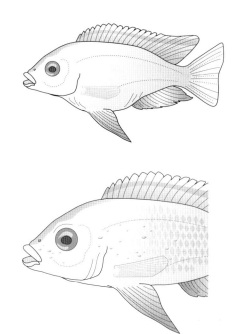

Cause: The exact cause of HLLE is poorly understood but it is generally thought to be environmental in nature, involving such parameters as improper water quality, nutritional deficiency, and generalized stress. It is particularly common in South American cichlids from soft and acidic regions that are being kept under hard, alkaline conditions, or fish such as Oscars that are being fed a diet solely composed of feeder goldfish. High nitrate levels and overcrowding are other predisposing factors. At one time it was thought to be caused by the flagellate *Hexamita*, but this has now been discounted.

Treatment: This condition has been arrested and reversed by improvements in water quality, performing more frequent and larger partial water changes, better diet, and eliminating overly aggressive fish from the aquarium.

Nematodes (Threadworms and Roundworms)

Symptoms: Gradual emaciation, sometimes in spite of a normal appetite. If the worms are present in large numbers the abdominal area will appear slightly distended, as if the fish has eaten a large meal. In my experience New World cichlids, particularly discus, eartheaters, and angelfish, are the most commonly affected.

Cause: Intestinal worms, particularly threadworms of the genus *Capillaria*.

Treatment: There are several effective vermifuge preparations sold at pet stores. Do not overdose, as they can be quite toxic if not used correctly. Another excellent treatment is adding fenbendazole (Panacur) to a frozen gel diet to achieve a concentration of 1 percent active ingredient. This drug must be obtained from a veterinarian. One feeding is adequate.

THE BEHAVIOR OF CICHLIDS

There is hardly another group of fish that has developed as rich a repertoire of complex behavior patterns as the cichlids. Undoubtedly, these traits have had much to do with the popularity of cichlids as aquarium fish.

The "Language" of Cichlids

Cichlids have several different means of conveying information to each other about their species, sex, and mood. These include coloration and color pattern, sound utterances and chemical signals, and complex behavior patterns. These behaviors may be so highly evolved that cichlids from different areas of the world cannot understand each other's "languages," leading to misunderstandings and fights if they are kept together in the same aquarium.

Coloration and Color Pattern

Coloration, along with body shape, is what helps a cichlid tell whether another fish is of the same species. In many cichlids the coloration of adult males and females differs, signaling gender as well. Coloration and color

The golden mojarra, Herichthys bocourti, is a large, biparentally custodial cichlid from Guatemala.

pattern are important in determining the course of a chance encounter between cichlids, for if their appearance is radically different, they will—assuming they are the same size—frequently ignore each other. On the other hand, two adult males of the same or very similar species might engage in aggressive behavior.

In many cases coloration or color pattern can rapidly change, signaling moods such as aggression, submission, fear, or readiness to spawn. Many cichlids develop a special coloration during the hours of darkness that closely approximates their fright pattern. Others, such as female *Apistogramma* spp., develop a distinctive color pattern when caring for their young.

A dramatic example of color change can be found in those cichlids where only the strongest and most dominant male in a territory exhibits fully developed coloration, the remainder closely approximating the colors of a female. The Lake Malawi species *Aulonocara jacobfriebergi* is a good example of this. If the dominant male is removed or should die, the next-ranking male quickly develops full coloration and takes on the role of the dominant fish.

Sound Utterances and Chemical Signals

It has long been known that cichlids are capable of producing sounds. These are usually uttered in connection with aggressive behaviors or during courtship, but their exact meanings are still not fully understood. Even less is known about the meaning of chemical signals, although it is known that some cichlids use chemical signals to indicate a readiness to spawn.

Territorial Behavior

Many cichlids are territorial only when adult or during their reproductive period, the rest of the time exhibiting a shoaling, or schooling,

behavior. Schooling behavior of young cichlids is probably protective in nature, making it difficult for a predator to concentrate on one particular fish in a milling shoal of fry.

Although a few cichlids, such as Lake Tanganyika's *Neolamprologus brichardi*, shoal in mixed-age groups that include tiny fry to adults, the vast majority of cichlids establish territories of some sort at the onset of adulthood and reproductive activity. Territories can be divided according to the role they serve. There may be feeding, courtship, and breeding territories.

Cichlids with specialized feeding habits most frequently defend an optimum feeding territory. For example, the algae-eating *Pseudotropheus* cichlids from Lake Malawi vigorously defend their feeding areas against all comers. Algae is a food that is low in nutritional value and often in short supply. Defending a productive patch against interlopers may mean the difference between adequate food or starvation. On the other hand, cichlids that feed on open-water plankton rarely defend a feeding territory.

Courtship and breeding territories are established by the vast majority of cichlid species and will be discussed more fully in the next chapter.

An aquarium divider is a practical way to spawn highly aggressive Victoria Basin cichlids. The holes in the divider permit the male to fertilize the female's eggs, while at the same time preventing the male from overly harassing, or even killing, the female. For more information, see Breeding Particularly Aggressive Species, page 55.

Aggressive Behavior

Assuming that your aquarium is large enough and furnished with adequate hiding places, fights between unevenly matched opponents are usually over quickly with little damage incurred by the weaker fish. The danger of prolonged violent fights is greater between evenly matched opponents.

Cichlid aggressive behavior usually starts with ritualized displays intended to intimidate one's opponent.

✔ Most common is the *lateral display* in which both fish position themselves broadside to each other while spreading their fins to their fullest, assuming their brightest colors, and beating their tails in a manner that sends a wave in the direction of the opponent.

✔ Another threat display is the *frontal display*. Here the gill covers are spread wide and the mouth held open, both increasing the apparent size of the head. If these symbolic, ritualized displays do not cause one of the fish to flee, actual fights may develop. Adversaries may grab each other by the mouth and twist and tussle in a wrestling match intended to demonstrate each fish's strength and endurance.

✔ Another common cichlid aggressive behavior is body ramming. Most frequently one or the other of these behaviors will cause one of the fish to flee. Prolonged fights of either type can cause severe damage to both combatants.

Caution! In the confines of an aquarium the loser cannot flee as far as in nature, and the winner may mercilessly pursue his former adversary to the point of death. If you notice severe persecution of any of your aquarium's inhabitants, either the aggressor or the subordinate fish should be promptly removed, or more adequate hiding places provided.

CICHLID REPRODUCTION

Most fish provide no care for their eggs or fry, but all known species of cichlids are noteworthy for their highly evolved parental behavior. The mating system, courtship, spawning, and brood care behaviors exhibited by cichlids are so varied and complex that an entire book could easily be devoted to this one aspect of cichlid biology. In the following pages we will attempt to summarize the most salient points.

Some cichlid species form pairs for the duration of a breeding cycle, while others are polygamous. They may lay and care for their eggs on an open substrate such as a leaf or rock, hide them in cavelike hidden recesses, or incubate them in their mouths. For convenience, cichlids that lay their eggs on exposed substrates are called *open substrate breeders*, while those that lay their eggs in rock caves or other natural retreats are referred to as *cave*, or *hidden substrate*, *breeders*.

Chromidotilapia guentheri *from West Africa. This species is a pair-forming mouthbrooder. Immediately after the female releases the eggs (below), the male (above) picks them up in his mouth.*

Mouthbrooders

Even the technique of mouthbrooding has variations. Some mouthbrooding cichlids take their eggs into their mouths immediately after they are laid. These are called *immediate*, *advanced*, or *ovophile mouthbrooders*. Others, referred to as *delayed*, *primitive*, or *larvaphile mouthbrooders*, care for their eggs in a typical substrate breeder fashion, then take the fry into their mouths after they hatch. Whether the male, female, or both sexes orally brood the eggs and/or fry is dependent upon the species. In all mouthbrooding species the fry are not released from the safety of the brooding parent's mouth until they are fully formed and ready to feed. Amazing as it may seem, most mouthbrooders "call" the young back to the safety of their mouths at the first sign of danger, even after they may have grown too large for them all to fit! The duration of this exceptional parental care varies among the mouthbrooding species.

Mating Systems

As we have seen, cichlids can be either monogamous or polygamous.

Monogamy

In monogamous cichlids a male and female first select each other as mates and then stay together while caring for their eggs and fry. These cichlids are referred to as *biparentally custodial* or as forming a *nuclear family*. A subdivision of this mating system is called the *paternal-maternal* system. Here, the female takes sole responsibility for the care of the eggs while the male protects the territory, but after the eggs hatch both parents share equally in the care of the fry.

Polygamy

Many cichlids' mating systems can be described as polygamous. In polygamous cichlids no true pair bond exists. Both male and female polygamous cichlids generally show no mate fidelity and will readily spawn with more than one mate during a breeding season. Polygamy in cichlids can take several forms

Harem polygamists: These are cichlids in which a single male controls a territory that is subdivided among a number of females, breeding with each of them in turn (example: genus *Apistogramma*). In general, brood care is exclusively maternal, the male's contribution limited to defense of his territory—and inadvertently, defense of the females and their fry. Most harem polygamists are cave spawners, and are characterized by extreme differences in size and color between the sexes This is known as *sexual dimorphism.*

Open polygamy: This describes the mating system where a male and female come together only for the spawning act. Many open polygamists are nonterritorial, spawning occurring anywhere that a sexually ready pair might meet, and after spawning the female leaves the male's territory (example: genus *Tropheus*). All cichlids that practice open polygamy are maternal mouthbrooders, the male making no contributions to the care of his progeny. In some open polygamous cichlids, groups of males establish their individual territories in close proximity, forming what is known as a *lek*, and then compete among themselves for the attention of any passing female.

Extended family: In a relatively few cichlids the young from previous spawns stay in the parents' territory and help in the care and protection of later broods. This can result in the formation of a large shoal of fish of mixed ages. Frequently only the dominant adult pair in the shoal will breed. This family pattern is practiced by some Lake Tanganyika hidden substrate breeders from the genera *Julidochromis* and *Neolamprologus*. Probably the best known of these is the Brichard's cichlid, *Neolamprologus brichardi*.

Any aquarist wishing to breed cichlids must be fully aware of the mating system employed by the species in question. For example, a common cause for failure in attempting to breed polygamous cichlids is keeping them in pairs and not as one male and a number of females. Without a number of females to divide the male's amorous advances, the usual result is a badly battered, or killed, female.

Courtship

Courtship serves two major functions. It is a means of advertising and evaluating the vigor, health, and suitability of another fish as a prospective breeding partner, and serves to synchronize their respective states of sexual readiness. Courtship is invariably more complex and prolonged in monogamous cichlids that form a close bond throughout a reproductive cycle than in polygamous or harem-forming species that associate briefly for egg laying.

Initiating Courtship

Depending on the species, one sex may initiate and court more heavily than the other. This is particularly true in both territorial and non-territorial polygamous species such as cichlids in the genera *Apistogramma* and *Cyprichromis*. In the former, it is the female that usually initiates courtship of the territorial male, while in open-water *Cyprichromis* species, a dominant male courts any nearby female. In species with pronounced sexual dimorphism it is generally the more colorful sex that initiates courtship. For instance, the courtship of both the South American cichlids of the genus *Crenicichla* (pike cichlids) and African cichlids of the genus *Pelvicachromis* is initiated by the female and designed to display her colorful, egg-laden abdomen. In cichlids without a pronounced difference of appearance between the sexes, both partners usually take equal part in the courtship.

Courtship might include, but not be limited to
✔ changes in color
✔ both lateral and open-mouth frontal displays
✔ jaw-locking wrestling matches that test a prospective mate's strength and stamina
✔ ritualized cleaning behavior of a potential spawning site.

The courtship of polygamous New and Old World mouthbrooders is usually much more simple, consisting of nothing more than the male spreading his fins and shaking himself in front of a female.

Stages of Courtship

The initial stages of courtship closely resemble early stages of aggressive behavior and both have probably developed from similar evolutionary behavior patterns. Furthermore, there is always the probability of courtship between unsuitable prospective mates escalating into outright battles that can result in the death of the weaker fish. Experienced aquarists are well aware that a major potential problem in the breeding of monogamous cichlids is obtaining a compatible pair, and then having the pair bond continue uninterrupted throughout the entire breeding cycle.

Breeding Particularly Aggressive Species

In the limited confines of an aquarium, males of some of the larger and more aggressive South American and African cichlids can be so domineering and aggressive toward any female that it is very difficult to establish a pair bond. Fortunately, there are a number of things that you can do to mitigate this situation.

Polygamous species: With polygamous species, such as the rock-dwelling mbuna cichlids of Lake Malawi (see page 78), heavily stocking the aquarium with numerous other fish will provide the aggressive male numerous targets on which to vent his hostility, and avoid having one fish become the constant target. Just remember not to overstock an aquarium beyond its carrying capacity. As mentioned earlier, if you are setting up a one-species breeding tank for polygamous cichlids, stock it with only one male and several females.

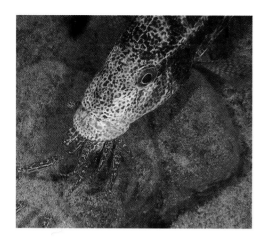

Monogamous species: When dealing with monogamous, substrate-spawning species a tried-and-true method of achieving a successful spawn is to divide the tank in half with a piece of light-diffusing panel known as egg crate material. A suitable spawning site should be placed with the female, but in close proximity to the divider. Both partners can see each other through this material but cannot come into actual contact. When the fish decide to spawn, enough of the male's sperm will pass through the divider to fertilize a large percentage of the eggs. A modification of this setup can be made for those cichlids where one of the females is decidedly smaller than the male. In this case an opening can be cut in the divider large enough to permit the smaller fish to pass through, but also permitting her to flee back to her side of the divider if the male becomes overly assertive. In this type of setup the spawning site is placed with the male.

TIP

Isolating Certain Breeding Pairs

If you happen to have particularly valuable or difficult-to-breed cichlids that bred in your community aquarium, it might be best not to disturb them. Instead, with as little commotion as possible, remove most of the other fish from the aquarium or isolate the breeding pair by partitioning the aquarium with a pane of glass.

✔ If you decide to partition the pair, be certain to give them adequate room. Depending on the filter system you are using, it might be necessary to add a filter to their portion of the aquarium.

✔ After the eggs have hatched and the young become free-swimming you can siphon the young from the community aquarium and raise them in a roomy nursery tank.

The cockatoo dwarf cichlid, **Apistogramma cacatuoides,** *is a polygynous species, one male controlling a territory that includes several females. (A male is shown.)*

Like all pike cichlids, **Crenicichla proteus** *form a nuclear family (female in foreground).*

Target fish: Adding a target fish or two (see page 14) can also be helpful by providing an alternative target for a male's aggression. This can be quite risky for the health of the target, but this danger can be eliminated by placing the target fish behind a glass partition within the aquarium. The important thing is that the cichlids can see the target; it is not necessary for them to actually be able to make contact with it.

Cichlid Eggs

It is true that larger fish of any one cichlid species produce more eggs than smaller fish, but the number, size, and color of the eggs produced is also a reflection of the breeding biology of the species in question. The size of the eggs increases, and the number decreases, roughly in proportion to the degree of parental care afforded the eggs and fry. Thus, highly specialized mouthbrooders, like the *Tropheus* cichlids from Lake Tanganyika, lay only 10 to

20 huge eggs that are about ¼ inch (6–7 mm) in diameter. In contrast to this, open substrate breeders may lay hundreds—or even thousands—of small eggs in a single spawn. These fish compensate for the greater predation inherent in their open spawning environment by producing larger numbers of eggs and fry. In addition, most open substrate breeders are biparentally custodial, with both parents present to guard and care for their spawn. Intermediate in the

The daffodil cichlid, a color variety of **Neolamprologus olivaceous,** *often form large extended families.*

number of eggs produced are the cave-spawning cichlids. It is true that most of these are not as large as some of the open substrate breeders, but size for size, their eggs tend to be fewer in number but still numerous.

An interesting phenomenon is that a large percentage of mouthbrooding and cave-spawning cichlids lay eggs that are distinctly colored. (See photo, page 60, bottom left.) The hue may vary from an opaque yolk color in many Rift lakes mouthbrooders, to a deep orange-red in Apistogrammas. The eggs of open substrate breeders, on the other hand, tend to be a camouflaging clear, tan or mud color.

The Breeding Tank

When conditions are right, cichlids will readily breed in a community aquarium. But since most cichlids are exceptionally aggressive toward other fish when defending their eggs and fry, the presence of a breeding pair of cichlids in a community aquarium can be anything but pleasant for the tank's other inhabitants. In addition, the constant distraction caused by the other fish frequently results in the cichlids abandoning or eating their spawn. It is therefore always a good idea to set up a special breeding aquarium for each species of cichlid you would like to spawn. Make certain that this aquarium is large enough to comfortably house the breeders and their young.

Equipment

The technical equipment for a breeding tank is similar to that used in a normal aquarium, namely adequate filtration, a heater and thermometer, and an aquarium light. The substrate, furnishings, and water quality should be suited to the species of cichlid that will inhabit the aquarium. Be particularly careful to use a filter that will not suck up the young, or place a foam rubber sleeve over the intake tubes. After the breeding aquarium is set up and the filter has cycled (see Filter Cycling, page 21), a breeding pair of biparentally custodial cichlids or one male and a number of females of a polygamous species should be placed in the aquarium. In addition to providing a selection of suitable spawning sites, provide plenty of hiding places in case the courtship becomes a bit stormy. These can be rock structures, pieces of PVC pipe, sections of tree roots, and plant thickets—plastic plants can be used with those cichlids that would destroy live ones.

Note: It should not be forgotten that a previously compatible pair of adult cichlids might become mutually aggressive when moved to another aquarium. It is always best when planning to breed a pair-forming cichlid to buy a group of half-grown fish and place these by themselves in what will hopefully become the breeding aquarium. Chances are that as they mature, at least one compatible pair will develop and you can then remove the rest. This might take longer than buying an adult pair, but there is a greater chance of success.

Spawning Sites

Substrate Breeders

Smooth, flat rocks are preferred by many open substrate spawners, such as African jewel fish (*Hemichromis* spp.) and the Central American genus *Thorichthys*. These fish will also frequently accept pieces of submerged bogwood for depositing their spawn. Provide a number

Various natural and artificial spawning structures.

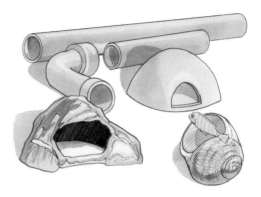

of these potential spawning sites in different sizes and locations so the breeding pair can select the one that most appeals to them.

Slate or broad-leaf plants: Pieces of slate positioned vertically are admirable spawning sites for those cichlids, such as discus and green chromides (*Etroplus suratensis*), that prefer to spawn on vertically oriented solid substrates, while the broad leaves of living or plastic plants are preferred by a smaller number of cichlids, most notably the ever-popular angelfish (which will also accept pieces of slate) and the lyre-tail checkerboard cichlid, *Dichrossus filamentosus*.

Clay flowerpots: Clay flowerpots are superb spawning sites for a large number of cave-spawning species. These can be positioned horizontally on their sides, or vertically with the bottom facing up. To create a more shallow cave a horizontally positioned flowerpot can first be split lengthwise, or partially buried in the aquarium gravel. For vertically oriented flowerpots the drain hole should be enlarged to a size that permits the female or both sexes to enter. In many cave-spawning dwarf cichlids the male releases his milt (sperm cells) just outside the cave's opening and it is the female's fin action that creates a current that brings the milt into the cave to fertilize the eggs. Caves can also be constructed from stones or made out of half a coconut shell with an entrance hole chipped out. A variation in cave-spawning behavior is seen in many Rift Lakes cichlids, such as the mbunas, that live and breed among piles of rocks. When

attempting to spawn these fish the breeding aquarium should be set up to duplicate such an environment.

Note: When using clay flowerpots, make certain that they are new and clean. Pots that have been previously used for houseplants may contain fertilizer salts and other harmful chemicals.

Mouthbrooders

Advanced mouthbrooders are generally not particular about spawning sites, but many prefer to spawn in pits they dig in flat, open areas of the gravel substrate. Notable exceptions are the rock-dwelling ovophile mouthbrooders from the African Rift Valley lakes that breed among piles of rocks. Delayed (larvaphile) mouthbrooders are more specific in their choice of a spawning site, most preferring to lay their adhesive eggs on a flat stone in the manner of open substrate breeders.

Encouraging Spawning

In nature there are certain conditions that have a stimulating effect on a cichlid's readiness to breed. Many cichlids breed at the

Top: Lateral and open mouth displays as seen in this pair of Crenichla proteus *are an integral part of cichlid courtship.*

Middle: Hemichromis stellifer, *like all West African red jewel fish species, are open substrate breeders. Jewel fish frequently spawn in a community aquarium where their extreme protectiveness of their eggs and fry may result in injuries to their tankmates.*

Bottom: Many Apistogrammas, including *Agassiz's dwarf cichlid, lay coral-red eggs. (Female shown.) A male is shown on the top of page 33.*

This female Biotoecus opercularis *has selected the roof of a clay flowerpot as a spawning site.*

When breeding particularly aggressive species, such as this pair of Tilapia buttikofferi, a modified egg-crate divider is often the best solution.

The Nicaragua cichlid, Hypsophrys nicaraguensis, lays nonadhesive eggs.

The convict cichlid, Archocentrus nigrofasciatus, becomes sexually mature well before attaining full size.

The altum angel, Pterophyllum altum, is the largest and most beautiful of its genus, but very delicate and rarely bred.

CHECKLIST

Rules for Raising Cichlid Fry

In raising cichlid fry there are a few rules that should be obeyed:

1 Feed several times daily; the bellies of the fry should always appear full and rounded.

2 Carefully siphon off any uneaten food and accumulated wastes on a daily basis.

3 Maintain optimum water quality by performing frequent partial water changes. Baby fish are particularly sensitive to poor water quality.

4 If the fry grow at an uneven rate, they should be sorted by size to prevent cannibalism.

5 Overcrowding will stunt a baby fish's growth; therefore do not permit the growing fry to overcrowd their aquarium. Either remove some of them to another growing tank, or use them as live food for your other fish. It is always best to raise a smaller number of healthy, non-stunted fish than risk losing all of them due to poor growing conditions.

onset of the rainy season when water quality improves and food sources become more abundant. You can simulate this by performing frequent partial water changes and increasing the variety and amount of foods offered. Live and frozen foods are particularly beneficial.

Other helpful techniques for cichlids that seem to get along fine but refuse to spawn are to raise the water temperature slightly and increase filtration. On the other hand, for those cichlids that normally inhabit shaded forest habitats (*Apistogramma, Nanochromis*, and others), but have been kept near 80°F (27°C), a slight cooling of the water to around 76°F (25°C) may simulate cooling rain and provide the triggering mechanism.

Raising the Fry

The major problem in raising a spawn of baby tropical fish is to provide them with an adequate amount of nourishing food small enough for them to eat. Fortunately for the aquarist, almost all cichlid fry are large enough to readily accept newly hatched brine shrimp nauplii and powder-fine dry foods as their first foods. Notable exceptions are the young of discus and uaru. In these fish the parents secrete a nourishing mucus over their bodies that serves as the food for their young for up to a couple of weeks. Raising fry of these species apart from their parents is very difficult at best. For virtually all other cichlids, brine shrimp nauplii is just about the best first food. The brine shrimp eggs (really cysts) and hatchers can be bought at your local pet shop and the eggs hatched at home. You can also easily construct a brine shrimp hatcher from a 2-liter plastic soft drink bottle (see page 63). As the fish grow larger, other frozen and dry foods of suitable size can be gradually substituted for the baby shrimp.

Constructing a Brine Shrimp Hatcher

Construction

1. With a sharp knife or scissors remove the bottom 4 inches (10 cm) from a 2-liter plastic soft drink bottle. This will form the stand.

2. Screw the cap on the top portion of the bottle and invert it into the stand you have just made.

3. Insert into the top portion of the bottle a length of rigid air line tubing attached to an air pump with a length of flexible air line tubing.

Use

1. Add the proper amount of water, salt, and eggs as specified on the egg container.

2. Turn up the air enough to keep all the eggs in suspension during the hatching process (24–48 hours depending on the temperature).

Collecting the Shrimp

1. Remove the air line. The eggshells will gradually float, and the shrimp will settle to the bottom of the hatcher.

2. Using a piece of air line tubing, siphon the shrimp through a fine mesh brine shrimp net (available at pet stores).

3. Rinse the shrimp to remove excess salt and feed to your fish.

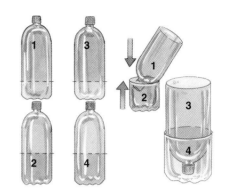

Construction

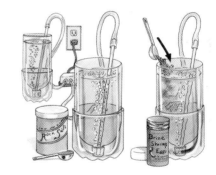

Add water, an air line, salt, and shrimp eggs.

Construction of a brine shrimp hatcher.

Collecting shrimp nauplii

The chichlid fauna of the Americas is a diverse lot that inhabits a wide variety of habitats and displays great variation in size, dietary preference, breeding biology, and ease of care.

Cichlids of North and Central America (Mesoamerica)

This grouping includes all those cichlids found from extreme south Texas through Central America to Panama. Although these cichlids are frequently referred to as being from Central America, by definition, Central America does not include Mexico, the home to many of these fish. A better term is Mesoamerican. Most Mesoamerican cichlids were formerly included in the genus *Cichlasoma*, and this is how they are listed in most older books. Recently this genus has been split into numerous smaller generic groupings; the exact number and validity of each is still a matter of debate.

In general, these cichlids are easily maintained and fed, preferring neutral to slightly alkaline water of medium hardness, and spacious quarters. The majority of these fish are

Discus fish secrete a nutritious body slime that serves as the first food for their fry.

prodigious diggers. Most are medium-large to large fish. The small firemouth (*Thorichthys meeki*) and its generic relatives, and the convict cichlid (*Archocentrus nigrofasciatus*) are notable exceptions. Some, such as the familiar Texas cichlid, *Herichthys cyanoguttatus*, develop distinctive contrasting color patterns at the onset of breeding. With the exception of a few cave spawners and the mouthbrooding *"Geophagus" crassilabrus*, Mesoamerican cichlids are biparentally custodial open substrate breeders. The Nicaragua cichlid, *Hypsophrys nicaraguensis*, is peculiar in being the only pit-spawning, nonmouthbrooding substrate spawner that lays nonadhesive eggs.

Males of many species are larger and more masculine in appearance, and develop elongated points to their dorsal and anal fins and a fatty hump on their head. Some genera, such as *Archocentrus* and *Herichthys*, are reproductively precocious, breeding long before achieving adult size. An interesting point is that many genera of Mexican and Central American cichlids have a characteristic metallic, silvery blue-green iris to their eyes.

Some Popular Mesoamerican Cichlids

Common name	Latin name	Adult size	Mating system*
Firemouth	Thorichthys meeki	6 inches (15 cm)	BC; OSS
Convict cichlid	Archcentrus nigrofasciatus	4.5–5.5 inches (12–14 cm)	BC; CS
Nicaragua cichlid	Hypsophrys nicaraguensis	males to 10 inches (25 cm) females smaller	BC; OSS
Pink-headed cichlid	Theraps synspilus	12 inches (30 cm)	BC; OSS
Black-belt	Theraps maculicauda	12 inches (30 cm)	BC; CS
Salvin's cichlid	Nandopsis salvini	6 inches (15 cm)	BC; OSS
Texas cichlid	Herichthys cyanoguttatus	10 inches (25 cm)	BC; OSS

*BC: Biparentally custodial; OSS: Open substrate breeder; CS: Cave spawner

Guapotes and Mojarras

This is a very heterogeneous group of fish. Some, such as the huge, predatory, fish-eating guapotes and mojarras of the genera *Nandopsis*, *Amphilophus*, and *Caquetia*, and the omnivorous red devil, *Amphilophus labiatus,* are just about as aggressive and territorial as a cichlid can get. They require huge aquariums, are gluttonous feeders, and are probably best relegated to the realm of public aquariums, where they make a wonderful display. A notable exception is the atypically small *Nandopsis salvini* (see photo, page 68), a gorgeous, surprisingly peaceful species that matures at 6 inches (15 cm). The two large guapotes kept with any frequency are the jaguar cichlid, *N. managuensis*, and Dow's cichlid, *N. dovii*. These are usually maintained in solitary confinement as special pets. Unfortunately, under such conditions there is no way to observe their interesting social behavior patterns.

Behavior	Notes
Quite peaceful except when breeding.	Highly recommended, as are all others in genus.
Quite aggressive for its size. Best kept in its own aquarium. Destroys plants.	Very easily bred. A good beginners' fish. An attractive albino form available.
Rather mild-mannered. Addicted to digging.	Lays nonadhesive eggs in sheltered gravel pits. Beautiful and highly recommended.
Suprisingly peaceful with cichlids of similar size and disposition, such as *H. nicaraguensis*, if given adequate room (at least 100 gallons—379 L).	Deservedly popular. Highly vegetarian. *T. fenestratus* and *hartwegi* require similar conditions and are equally beautiful.
More feisty than previous species, particularly when spawning. Intolerant of conspecifics.	Requires a large aquarium. Attains full color only at maturity. Does well with other *Theraps* species
Doesn't dig or bother plants. Aggressive only when spawing. Hardy.	Adults develop red flanks. Foods rich in carotenes, such as krill, will enhance their colors. Males are more brightly colored.
Herichthys spp. are generally aggressive and intolerant of other cichlids.	The only cichlid native to the United States. Easily bred. Often confused with related Mexican *H. carpintis*.

Firemouths and Their Kin

On the other hand, members of the genus *Thorichthys*, such as the firemouth, *T. meeki*, when not breeding, are among the most peaceful of medium-size cichlids. They do very well with other cichlids of similar disposition and size, or in a mixed community aquarium with appropriate noncichlid fish. They tend to be habitual diggers, but do not intentionally destroy or uproot plants. These cichlids have very striking threat displays. The gill covers are flared to display their ocellated black false eyespots, while the brilliantly colored branchiostegal membranes are extended. In nature, *Thorichthys* spp. are substrate-sifting cichlids, feeding upon small insect larvae and other animal life forms that they uncover. In the aquarium they are easily satisfied with the usual assortment of prepared and frozen foods.

The highly contrasting color pattern of this Texas cichlid, Herichthys cyanoguttatus, *indicates its readiness to spawn. This is the only cichlid naturally occurring within the continental United States.*

Larger Herbivores

The cichlids revolving around the large and usually deep-bodied fish of the genus *Theraps* (sometimes subdivided into *Theraps* and *Paratheraps*) are deservedly among the most popular of the larger cichlids, and make beautiful and satisfactory aquarium fish if you have the room to properly house them. These fish are

Salvin's cichlid, Nandopsis salvini, *is one of the smallest and most beautiful of its genus.*

highly vegetarian and make short work of tender aquarium plants. Make certain that their diet contains adequate vegetable matter, but be warned. Although these fish are only moderately aggressive to other species, adults can be highly intolerant of others of their own species. For that reason it is best to keep only one adult specimen of any *Theraps* in a cichlid community aquarium, and as with all cichlids, give them ample room. Taken as a group, *Theraps* cichlids have proven rather difficult to breed in an aquarium. Undoubtedly, a major reason has been the difficulty of getting them to form a stable pair bond within the size limits of the average home aquarium. However, once a compatible pair is established, these fish can prove very prolific and are excellent parents. For the aquarist who desires a large mixed cichlid aquarium, these Mesoamerican species are sure to please.

South American Cichlids

Since the first imports in the early years of the tropical fish hobby, South American cichlids have been popular with aquarists worldwide. As a matter of fact, the angelfish, Oscar, and discus are arguably the most popular aquarium cichlids, and all are South American. Although many South American cichlids are medium to large in size, they vary from downright huge to dwarf species that are full grown at 1½ inches (3.7 cm). Some are nasty, aggressive species that are prodigious diggers and destroy or uproot plants, but many others are mild-mannered, beautiful fish suitable for a community, or a mixed cichlid aquarium. It should be noted that the revision of the genus *Cichlasoma* affected generic concepts of South American cichlids as significantly as those from Central America.

Diet: Just about all South American cichlids readily accept the usual array of dry and frozen foods. Notable exceptions are the highly piscivorous peacock basses and pike cichlids that prefer live fish, and the rarely kept plankton-filtering basketmouths of the genus *Chaeto-branchus*. Although some South American cichlids will consume tender plants, just about the only truly vegetarian species kept with any regularity is the uaru. In its dietary habits, this large and elegant blackwater fish can be compared to an aquatic goat!

Reproduction: Within the South American cichlids we find many different reproductive modalities. There are both cave and open substrate spawners, as well as immediate and delayed mouthbrooders. Although the majority are monogamous, polygamy is not uncommon, and is almost the rule with the dwarf species. In general, most do well with a water temperature near 80°F (27°C), a few degrees warmer for breeding. Exceptions to this are the Gymogeophagines that come from a more southerly range and can tolerate it a bit cooler, and the discus that prefers water temperatures in the low to mid 80s°F (28–29°C).

Among this region's cichlids are some of the most adaptable and easily maintained species as well as some of the most challenging. Aquarists should be aware that a majority of South American cichlids are quite sensitive to dissolved nitrogenous metabolites and associated bacteria. This is particularly true for the many desirable species originating in the virtually sterile, acidic, and soft blackwater areas.

Water conditions: Understanding the diverse water conditions found in South America is essential for properly caring for these cichlids. Most of the major waterways of South America

Pink-headed cichlids, Theraps synspilum, *are striking but large, highly herbivorous fish that require large aquariums with good filtration.*

can be classified as either white or black water. White water, such as that found in the Amazon River's main channel, is turbid with eroded silts and clays, moderately rich in nutrients, close to neutral in pH, and fairly soft (70–120 ppm). Black water, on the other hand, is free of sediment, but stained a deep brown from tannins leached from decaying vegetation, and resembles strong tea. Black waters are nutrient poor, normally very soft (less than 15 ppm hardness), and moderately to extremely acidic (pH 4.5–5.5). As a consequence of the nutrient deficiency and acidity, black waters are almost sterile. It should therefore come as no surprise that blackwater cichlids are more delicate and demanding as aquarium fish. Under less than ideal conditions, they are very prone to head and lateral line erosions (see page 46) and various bacterial infections.

Giant Cichlids

The undisputed giants of the South American cichlids are the various peacock basses of the genus *Cichla*, the largest of which, *C. temensis,* can reach a length of nearly 3 feet (91 cm), making it one of the two largest cichlids in the world. Within their native ranges they are highly esteemed as game and food fish, and for these reasons have been stocked in climatically suitable areas of the world, most often to the detriment of the native fish population! Although small specimens are frequently seen at pet shops, they will quickly outgrow even the largest of home aquariums. They are also notoriously reluctant to accept anything but live fish as food.

Dwarf Cichlids

At the other end of the size scale are the charming, and often challenging, dwarf cichlids (genera *Apistogramma*, *Microgeophagus*, *Taeniacara*, *Biotoecus*, *Dichrossus*, and a few others), most of which mature at under 3 inches (7.6 cm) for males, and significantly less for females. Possibly the most frequently available of these is the delightful but rather delicate blue ram, *Microgeophagus ramirezi* (see page 8). Most of the others must be obtained from specialty breeders, and are well worth searching for. Although the ram is a monogamous substrate breeder, all the others, with the possible exception of *Biotoecus* that frequently behaves in a monogamous fashion, are territorial, cave-spawning, harem breeders. For a would-be cichlid aquarist with room for a fish tank not exceeding 10 gallons (38 L) in size, the blue ram and the hardier Apistogrammas are perfect choices. Although small in size, they embody all the interesting behavioral and breeding traits of their larger cousins, are beautiful in color and form, generally peaceful, and do not rearrange an aquarium's architecture nor uproot plants. But be forewarned: Most of these dwarf cichlids only grudgingly accept flake foods, and for proper maintenance require small

frozen or living food items. Newly hatched brine shrimp and frozen bloodworms are particularly relished. It should be reemphasized that blackwater species are particularly delicate, and it is prudent to research the natural environment of any of them before acquiring them.

Eartheaters

The eartheaters of the genera *Geophagus*, *Satanoperca*, and *Gymnogeophagus*, as well as the various smaller acaras are made to order for those aquarists desiring a relatively peaceful community aquarium of medium to medium-large cichlids. The eartheaters received their common name from their habit of constantly rooting in the substrate looking for food. Sand, mud, and gravel are taken in their mouth and after removing anything edible, expelled through their gills. Most have evolved elongated snouts to aid in this behavior. Within this group are monogamous substrate breeders, as well as immediate and delayed mouthbrooders. A few are even polygamous. In the monogamous mouthbrooders either or both sexes may perform the task of oral brooding. If they have one drawback, it is an intolerance of deteriorating water quality, a situation that quickly expresses itself in head and lateral line erosions. As is the rule with South American cichlids, whitewater species, such as *S. jurupari*, are less sensitive than their blackwater relatives.

Acaras

Acara is the name given to those cichlids formerly belonging to the genus *Aequidens*, a group that has now been divided into a number of separate genera. The so-called smiling acaras (newly erected genus *Laetacara*), the delayed mouthbrooding acaras of the new genus *Bujurquina*, and the blue acaras still tentatively remaining in the genus *Aequidens*, are all highly recommended. With the exception of a few of the blue acara lineage, such as the large, green terror ("*A.*" *rivulatus*) (see page 36), all are small to medium-size fish that do well in a community aquarium housing cichlids and other fish species of similar size, disposition, and requirements. Both the eartheaters and the acaras rarely bother aquatic plants, but it is suggested that a few small stones be placed around their roots to prevent them from being accidentally displaced by the feeding behavior of the Geophagines.

Keyhole cichlids: An extremely peaceful smaller member of this assemblage is the key-hole cichlid, *Cleithracara maroni*. This long-popular, gentle, and shy substrate-spawning fish from the Guianas rarely grows larger than 4 inches (10 cm) and does best in a planted community aquarium with other nonaggressive fish.

Pike Cichlids

Pike cichlids, genus *Crenicichla* (see pages 37 and 57), form a very distinctive and frequently maligned group that varies in size from under 4 inches (10 cm), to over 1 foot (30 cm). They have an elongated torpedo shape and fish-eating habits. Fortunately, with a bit of training they are easily weaned over to nonliving foods. Most are sexually dimorphic, the females generally the more colorful. All are biparentally custodial cave spawners with a paternal-maternal family pattern, and are devoted parents. Care of the eggs and newly hatched fry is performed by the female while the male defends their territory. After the young become free-swimming they are cared for by both parents. These fish are often undeservedly accused of unrestrained aggression and thuggery. It is true that they are intolerant of other pike cichlids, and breeding pairs are extremely protective of their spawn, but single specimens are remarkably peaceful when kept with fish too large to swallow. As an added bonus, pike cichlids ignore aquarium plants.

Miscellaneous Cichlids

South America is also home to a number of rather large (over 8 inches—20 cm) cichlids. Although some, such as those of the genus *Cichlasoma*, and the ever-popular Oscar (see page 12), can be highly territorial and aggressive, there are numerous others that are much more mild-mannered and excellent candidates for a large community cichlid aquarium. Among the most beautiful and satisfactory are the chocolate cichlid, *Hypselecara temporalis* (see page 12), and the severums, *Heros severus,* and its generic relatives. In these species the sexes are rather similar, but adult males have elongated dorsal and anal fin points, and male chocolate cichlids develop a large frontal hump on the head giving them a "bull-headed" look. *H. severus* is available in both wild-colored and a mutational golden (xanthistic) form. These species are biparentally custodial open substrate breeders.

The last of the South American cichlids that must be mentioned is that artificial group comprising the angelfish (genus *Pterophyllum*) (see pages 4 and 61), festive cichlids (*Mesonauta* spp.), discus fish (*S. aequifasciatus* and *discus*), and the uaru. In nature the first three are very social, living in loose assemblages among submerged brush and semiaquatic plants. These fish are all peaceful species and should not be kept with more aggressive cichlids. All of the mentioned species are monogamous, open substrate spawners, and except for the highly vegetarian uaru, do not dig up or destroy plants.

CICHLIDS OF AFRICA

Africa has more species of cichlids than any other continent. In fact, Lake Malawi has more species of cichlids than all of South America! It is convenient to divide Africa's cichlid fauna into two major groupings based on their aquarium husbandry requirements. These are the riverine species from mainly West and North Africa, and those that inhabit the African Great Lakes, most notably Malawi, Tanganyika, and Victoria.

West and North African Riverine Cichlids

The rivers and streams of Africa are home to numerous species of cichlids that belong to a number of distinct evolutionary lineages. Of these, most of the popular aquarium species are small to medium-size fish that belong to the following major groups—the tilapines, hemichromines, and chromidotilapias—with a few haplochromines thrown in for good measure.

Tilapines

Tilapines are well represented in the fauna of these regions. Although highly valued as food fish, most of the larger, more typical species of the genera *Tilapia, Oreochromis,*

The bumpheaded cichlid, Steatocranus casuarius, lacks bright colors but is an interesting bottom-dwelling species from the Zaire River.

and *Saratherodon* have not achieved much popularity within the hobby, probably a result of their unmanageable size and frequently less than spectacular coloration.

One fish derived from a tilapine ancestor that has achieved a modicum of popularity is the bump-head cichlid, *Steatocranus casuarius.* This bottom-dwelling fish inhabits the rapids of the lower Zaire (formerly Congo) River. As an adaption to its benthic way of life, its swim bladder is greatly reduced in size. Males grow larger than females, reaching a length of 4.5 inches (11 cm), and develop a pronounced hump on the forehead. They are territorial, monogamous cave spawners and intolerant of other bottom-dwelling species. The young are large and easily raised. These very interesting fish are easily fed and adaptible to pH and water hardness, but require good water quality and high levels of dissolved oxygen. Other species in this unique genus have similar requirements but are rarely imported.

Hemichromines

As a result of their flashy coloration these feisty, small to medium size, mainly West African cichlids are known as jewelfish. All are hardy, easily fed, monogamous, open substrate breeders that ignore plants. They are adaptable to water chemistry, doing well in soft to moderately hard water of reasonable quality. Like the majority of cichlids, they thrive at a temperature of 75–80°F, with an increase to the low 80s°F (29°C) for breeding.

The more brightly colored, smaller species, such as the various red jewelfish, *H. cristatus* and its close relatives, and the even smaller and more peaceful dwarf jewelfish, *Anomalochromis thomasi*, are popular and highly recommended aquarium fish. Breeding pairs are quite aggressive in the defense of their young, so it is recommended that they be bred in a tank of their own or a very spacious community aquarium. Provide plenty of hiding places since males can be quite aggressive toward females, even after a pair bond has formed. Up to 500 eggs are laid in the open on smooth stones. These hatch in about 72 hours and the fry start to feed after an additional week. The fry are large enough to accept brine shrimp nauplii as a first food and are easily reared. When sorting the young, be aware that the males grow faster and larger than the females.

Chromidotilapias

Of the numerous cichlids belonging to this lineage, only a few of the dwarf species from the genera *Pelvicachromis* and *Nanochromis*, plus one or two larger *Chromidotilapia* have achieved any degree of popularity. In all species the males are larger and have longer fins than their more colorful mates. Their aquarium must be equipped with excellent biological filtration as all chromidotilapias are highly intolerant of dissolved nitrogenous metabolites.

All *Pelvicachromis* do well and regularly spawn in a community aquarium, but can become a bit territorial when spawning. They are monogamous cave spawners; the female cares for the eggs but both parents protect the free-swimming young. Digging is restricted to the vicinity of the spawning site and plants are ignored.

Kribensis: Probably the most popular West African cichlid, and one of the most frequently kept of all cichlids is the kribensis, *P. pulcher* (see photos, pages 16 and 77). Factors that have contributed to its popularity are its gorgeous colors and small adult size of only 3½ inches (9 cm) for males, one-third smaller for females. Adding to its assets are its hardiness, ease of breeding, and peaceful disposition. Although adaptable to pH and hardness, the kribensis and its relatives are highly intolerant of declining water quality and dissolved metabolites. To avoid a skewed sex ratio in the young, be certain that the pH is maintained close to neutral.

Different strains of this fish differ somewhat in the amount of red and the number of eyespots in the dorsal and tail, but all are highly attractive. The kribensis is the only member of its genus to be imported and commercially bred in any number. This is unfortunate, since all the other members of this genus would make equally beautiful aquarium fish. It is hoped that this situation will be rectified in the future.

Nudiceps: Of the roughly one dozen species in the genus *Nanochromis*, only one, the nudiceps, *N. parilius*, can be considered well established in the hobby. This slender and highly attractive dwarf cichlid is found in rapidly flowing sections of the Zaire River Basin and is particularly sensitive to declining water quality. Males are larger than the more colorful females, reaching a length of 3 inches (8 cm). A characteristic of this species is the prominent ovipositor of adult females, even when they are not in breeding condition. This bottom-dwelling cave spawner excavates retreats and breeding areas under rocks or pieces of wood. This digging may inadvertently uproot some plants. Males are highly intolerant of each other, and can be rough on the females and other bottom-dwelling species. Depending on conditions, this fish can behave as a monogamous or harem polygamous breeder.

Other cichlids in this genus that are occasionally available are *N. dimidiatus* and *N. transvestitus*. Both are beautiful but rather delicate; the former requires soft, slightly acid conditions, the latter slightly alkaline water of moderate hardness.

Günther's mouthbrooder: The final chromidotilapian species that can be considered a standard in the hobby is *Chromidotilapia guentheri*, known as Günther's mouthbrooder, or the mouthbrooding kribensis (see page 52). In contrast to the previously discussed species from this lineage, this fish is a monogamous, immediate mouthbrooder, and at an adult length of 7 inches (18 cm) for the male and a bit smaller for the female, cannot be considered a dwarf cichlid. Although its coloring is slightly reminiscent of the kribensis, the conspicuous metallic gold border to the dorsal fin is unique. An unusual feature of this fish is that it is generally the male that orally incubates the eggs, but after the fully developed fry are released, both parents permit them to return to the safety of their mouths when danger threatens.

This is an easily satisfied, peaceful cichlid that is adaptable to a wide range of pH and water hardness, as long as extremes are avoided. Except when breeding, it does well in a community aquarium with other relatively nonaggressive African or neotropical cichlids of similar requirements. Although this fish does not eat plants, it is advisable to place a few small stones around the bases of rooted aquarium plants to prevent them from being dislodged by the fish's digging activities.

Haplochromines

The vast majority of haplochromine cichlids are inhabitants of the African Great Lakes, and will be discussed in greater detail in the next section, but there are several non-lake-dwelling forms that have become established in the hobby. Of these, the dwarf mouthbrooders of the genus *Pseudocrenilabrus* are probably the most popular. When the Egyptian mouthbrooder, *P. multicolor,* was first imported from the Nile River around 1930, it was the first mouthbrooding aquarium fish to enter the hobby, and created quite a sensation. Almost every relatively knowledgeable home aquarist had to obtain a pair of these small and easily bred fish just to prove to himself or herself that the female really did incubate her eggs within her mouth! At present, *P. multicolor* and its even more brightly colored relative, *P. philander*, are being commercially bred, but their popularity has been largely overshadowed by their larger and more flashy Malawian haplochromine relatives. This is unwarranted, because these are hardy and very beautiful small cichlids that are well suited to the cichlid novice. They are polygamous, maternal mouthbrooders, and very easily bred. The eggs are laid

Hemichromis letourneaux is one of the less commonly seen species of red jewel fish.

in a gravel pit that the male excavates, and the female takes them into her mouth immediately after they have been fertilized. Incubation lasts about ten days and the young continue to use the female's mouth as a retreat for about a week longer. Even though male Egyptian mouthbrooders are full grown at a bit less than 3 inches (8 cm), they can be very aggressive toward other males and unreceptive females. A breeding group should therefore be given a tank of at least 20-gallon (76-L) capacity that is furnished with plenty of hiding places.

The leleupi, Neolamprologus leleupi, is one of the most attractive of the Lake Tanganyika lamprologines.

Cichlids of the African Great Lakes

Of the many East and North African lakes, only three can be considered important in the tropical fish hobby. These are Lakes Malawi and Tanganyika located within the Great Rift Valley, and the more northern Lake Victoria. Due to their different geological histories, the water quality of the Rift Valley lakes differs dramatically from that of Lake Victoria, located outside of the rift. Understanding the waters of these lakes is essential for successful aquarium maintenance of their fish faunas.

The Rift Valley is a long depression, or tear, in the earth's crust caused by the spreading of tectonic plates. Over most of Lakes Malawi and Tanganyika's long geological history they have had no outlets. Over millions of years the combination of mineral-laden streams flowing into these lakes combined with the evaporation of water from them has resulted in highly mineralized and alkaline water conditions. These two lakes are also known for their great clarity and chemical stability.

On the other hand, the enormous Lake Victoria is located within the shallow basin of a geological uplift, and excess water leaves this lake via the Victoria Nile, eventually entering the Nile River proper. Because this lake is not located within a closed basin, its waters are not nearly as hard and alkaline as those of Rift Valley lakes and it experiences fluctuations in both pH and hardness related to seasonal rainfall patterns.

Lake Malawi

It has been estimated that this lake is home to up to 800 species of cichlids, many still awaiting

Adult female nudiceps, Nanochromis parilius, are unusual in always showing an extended ovipositor.

Pelvicachromis pulcher, known as the kribensis, is by far the most popular of the African riverine cichlids.

formal description. All but five are of the haplochromine lineage and endemic (found nowhere else) to its waters. Even more amazing is that all of these endemic cichlids are thought to have been derived from a single ancestor (monophyletic). The classification of all the Great Lakes cichlids is in a major state of flux, with generic and species names constantly changing and new species being regularly described.

All Malawian cichlids are extremely sensitive to dissolved metabolites and high nitrate levels. For successful aquarium maintenance they require hard and alkaline water conditions (pH 7.5–8.5; dH 10–15°) and a temperature near 80°F (27°C). The waters of this lake are very uniform in quality, and in captivity its fish are highly intolerant of rapid fluctuation in water temperature, pH, or hardness. Although frequent partial water changes are mandatory in order to maintain the requisite high water quality, these should therefore be frequent and small rather than infrequent and large.

Except for one nonendemic species of the genus, *Tilapia*, all Lake Malawi cichlids are openly polygamous maternal mouthbrooders.

Most are moderately to strongly aggressive, males being particularly intolerant of males of their own species and to only a lesser degree similar-looking males of other species. Heavy stocking can minimize aggression, but excellent biological filtration and frequent small water changes are mandatory for this to succeed. To maximize breeding it is best to keep a group of one male and a number of females in a tank of their own. The size of the aquarium needed depends upon the size and number of fish in the breeding group. A 20–30-gallon (75–114-L) aquarium will suffice for a small species, but much larger housing will be required by the more robust Malawian cichlids. If you prefer a Lake Malawi cichlid community aquarium, make certain it is not less than 100 gallons (379 L) in size, that you do not mix relatively peaceful species with those known for their aggressiveness, and that you do not place in it more than a single male of any one species. Contrary to the norm with aquarium fish, Malawian cichlids will frequently grow larger in captivity than in the wild. In the confines of an aquarium many of these cichlids will hybridize. The chances of this

Comparisons of Lakes Malawi, Tanganyika, and Victoria

	Lake Malawi	Lake Tanganyika	Lake Victoria
Size	11,400 square miles (29,604 sq km)	13,124 square miles (34,000 sq km)	26,500 square miles (68,635 sq km)
Depth	2,310 feet (704 m)	4,823 feet (1,470 m)	305 feet (93 m)
pH	7.7–8.6	8.6–9.5	7.1–9.0
Hardness	6–10°dH	10–13°dH	2–8°dH
Temperature	73–82°F (23–28°C)	78–80°F (26–27°C)	73–78°F (23–26°C)
Estimated age	1–3 million years	possibly 10–20 million years	between 250,000–700,000 years
Elevation above sea level	1,554 feet (474 m)	2,535 feet (773 m)	3,720 feet (1,134 m)

happening can be greatly minimized by not mixing species of similar appearance.

Based on appearance, behavior, and biology, Lake Malawi haplochromine cichlids can be divided into two major groups: the mbuna group and the "Haplochromis," or utaka, group.

Mbunas: The mbunas comprise an easily recognized group of approximately 12 genera as remarkable for their brilliant coloration as much as for their incessant activity and aggressive nature. Many of the most popular aquarium species belong to the genera *Melanochromis, Labidochromis, Labeotrophis, Pseudotropheus,* and *Metriaclima* (the last considered by some as part of the genus *Pseudotropheus*). Mbuna, meaning rockfish in the Chitonga language, accurately describes the habitat preference of the vast majority of these fish. Females and young are usually some shade of yellow, blue, or brown, but as the males mature their coloration becomes distinctly different from that of their mates. A characteristic often seen in the haplochromines in general, which is particularly well developed in most mbunas, is the presence of yellow or orange spots resembling eggs on the male's anal fin that in many species play a role in their reproductive biology.

An aquarium meant to house mbuna cichlids should be liberally furnished with piles of rocks arranged to form numerous caves and passageways. As these fish are prodigious diggers, be certain that all rock structures are stable and rest firmly on the aquarium's bottom. There is no need for live plants, as they are lacking in their natural habitat, and if used, will probably be quickly eaten by these highly herbivorous fish. Pay particular attention to the selection of species for a community mbuna aquarium, and do not attempt to mix the smaller and/or more peaceful species with those known for unmitigated territorial aggression. A few of the more peaceful mbunas are the rusty cichlid, *Iodotropheus sprengeri*, Aurora cichlid, *Metriaclima* (*Pseudotropheus*) *aurora*, *Pseudotropheus flavus*, and many of the *Labidochromis*. For more detailed information refer to the books listed in Information, page 92.

Although a few mbunas are piscivorous in nature, the majority feed in the wild on algae and associated microinvertebrates, or are planktonic micropredators. Under aquarium conditions all mbunas have healthy appetites and will devour just about anything edible. To prevent digestive disturbances they should be fed small meals several times a day incorporating dry, fresh, and frozen foods rich in vegetable matter. Foods low in roughage, such as beef heart, should be avoided.

Mbunas breed readily in aquariums, with the spawning act occurring within the male's territory. Females take their eggs into their mouths immediately after they are laid. The female then either mouths the male's vent or the eggspots on his anal fin, which stimulates him to discharge sperm. As she inhales the cloud of milt the eggs are fertilized within her mouth. At 82°F (28°C), development of the eggs takes approximately 21 days, but the duration of post-release brood care varies among the different species. The released fry are more than large enough to immediately devour brine shrimp nauplii and finely powdered dry foods. If your aquarium has plenty of hiding places, and you provide adequate food for the young, a large percentage of the young should survive.

Haplochromis group: Most of the remaining 200 or so haplochromine cichlids of Lake Malawi were formerly included in the genus *Haplochromis*, a taxonomic grouping that has now been divided into approximately 40 separate genera! It should be obvious to the reader that a group as large, diverse, and popular as these fish cannot be covered with any degree of completeness in such a small book. Instead, I will attempt to provide some general guidelines.

These fish inhabit open water, or regions where sandy and rocky areas meet, and their aquarium should be set up to duplicate such an environment. They vary in size from species that mature at 4 inches (10 cm) to those that grow to well over 1 foot (30 cm). The natural dietary preferences of these fish vary greatly among the different genera and species. For example, the popular peacock cichlids of the genus *Aulonacara* are planktonic micropredators, while the larger *Nimbochromis*, *Scianochromis,* and *Stigmachromis* are basically piscivores. However, under aquarium conditions these fish readily accept the usual assortment of dry and frozen foods. They particularly relish the frozen and freeze-dried krills, and as an added bonus these foods are rich in natural color-enhancing precursors. These cichlids are quite subject to the digestive disturbance known as Malawi bloat, and it is recommended that they be offered several small feedings daily, rather than one big meal. All these cichlids require large and spacious aquariums and are even more sensitive than mbunas to dissolved metabolic wastes. Frequent small water changes and excellent biological filtration are essential for their survival. Unless your aquarium is really huge and deep (over 200 gallons [757 L] and 2 feet [61 cm] deep) it is not advisable to mix them with the aggressive and frenetically active mbunas. The females of many species of haplochromines are silver with darker vertical bars and are very difficult to tell apart,

Labeotrophis fuellerborni.

A male **Melanochromis johanni.**

and under aquarium conditions hybridization is a common occurrence. To prevent this, do not mix species of similar size and color in the same tank, or better still, set up a separate breeding aquarium containing a single male and a small group of females for each species you wish to reproduce. If you are planning a mixed "*Haplochromis*" community aquarium, remember that adult males are usually very intolerant of other males of their species, or the males of other species that have a similar appearance. You should also research the disposition and ultimate size of any species before adding it to your aquarium.

Lake Tanganyika

With a depth of 4,823 feet (1,470 m) Lake Tanganyika is the second-deepest lake in the world; only Lake Baikal in Russia is deeper. Compared with Lake Malawi, Lake Tanganyika is older, larger, twice as deep, harder and more alkaline, and experiences less fluctuation in water temperature (see table, page 78).

Lake Tanganyika is home to about 300 species of fish, over 220 of which are cichlids. All except one of these are found nowhere else on earth. There are a number of major differences between the cichlids of Lake Malawi and Lake Tanganyika. Of primary importance is their evolutionary biology. Whereas all the cichlids of Lake Malawi (except for the few tilapias) have evolved from a single ancestral species, those of Lake Tanganyika have a *polyphyletic* origin, having been derived from several distinct ancestors. At present, 12 distinct lineages have been identified, four of which have attained great popularity within the hobby. These are the Lamprologini, Cyprichromini, Ectodini, and Tropheini.

Reproduction: The reproductive modalities of Lake Tanganyika cichlids are also more varied than those of their Malawian relatives. All the nontilapine cichlids of Lake Malawi are polygamous maternal mouthbrooders, but in Lake Tanganyika we find both maternal and biparental mouthbrooders, open substrate breeders, and cave spawners. A unique group of cave spawners has come to utilize empty snail shells as their spawning site.

Water: Possibly as a result of the stability of Lake Tanganyika's water with regard to its temperature and chemical makeup, its fish lack the ability to cope with sudden environmental changes, and do not take well to large partial

A male electric blue hap, Scianochromis
fryeri *(known more commonly as*
Haplochromis ahli) *is one of the most
spectacularly colored of all cichlids.*

A large aquarium is required for the
venustus, Nimbochromis venustus, *a
species that reaches 10 inches (25 cm)
in length.*

water changes. In addition, all Tanganyikan cichlids are extremely sensitive to ammonia and
nitrite poisoning. It is therefore mandatory that
adequate attention be given to management of
the nitrogen cycle, and periodic partial water
changes are limited to no more than 10–15
percent of the aquarium's volume. As far as pH
and hardness are concerned, there is no need to
try and duplicate the natural water of the lake.
All these cichlids require is that it be alkaline
(pH 7.5–8.5) and moderately hard. Just be certain
that they are slowly acclimated to your aquarium's water chemistry, and that it remains stable.

If your tap water happens to be soft, it can easily
be adjusted by the addition of any of several
brands of Malawi and Tanganyika salts available
at most pet stores. A bit of attention should also
be paid to the water temperature. For general
maintenance 75–82°F (24–27°C) is satisfactory,
but the chance of reproduction is increased at
the warmer end of this range. These fish do
poorly when kept for prolonged periods of time
below 72°F (22°C) or above 85°F (29°C).

Lamprologines: The lamprologines are the
most specious group of fish within the lake,
comprising over 50 percent of its endemic cichlid

*The bulging throat
of this female
Cynotilapia afra
indicates that it is
incubating eggs.*

fish fauna. Lamprologines are among the most colorful, hardy, and readily bred of Tanganyikan cichlids. They vary in size from 2-inch (5.1-cm) dwarf shell dwellers to robust 12-inch (30-cm) predators. As can be expected, most of the numerous species popular in the hobby are dwarf to small in size.

As far as is known, they are all hidden substrate spawners. Under certain conditions a relatively few species (*Neolamprologus brichardi*, *Julidochromis* spp.) permit their young to remain within their breeding territory, resulting in the formation of a large group of fish of various ages that all contribute to the defense of the smaller fry. It is also interesting to note that several species that behave in the wild as monogamous breeders switch to a polygamous system in an aquarium when there is an excess of females.

A particularly charming group of lamprologines are the dwarf shell dwellers, such as *Lamprologus signatus*, *L. ocellatus*, and *Neolamprologus similis*. The last-named species is the smallest known cichlid within the lake, males full grown at 1.5 inches (3.8 cm), females $\frac{1}{2}$ inch (1.3 cm) smaller. In the wild these fish live over open sandy flats and utilize the snail shells both as a retreat and for breeding. They are mostly monogamous but certain species practice harem polygamy. The eggs are invariably deposited deep within an empty snail shell and cared for by the female, the male defending the territory. Some even bury their shell, leaving only its orifice exposed. A pair can be successfully maintained and bred in aquariums as small as 5 to 10 gallons (19–38 L) as long as attention is paid to maintaining satisfactory water quality.

Most of the remaining Tanganyikan cichlids are maternal mouthbrooders. Some of these, such as the goby cichlids belonging to the tribe Eretmodini (*Eretmodus*, *Tanganicodus*, and so on) are monogamous, but the vast majority are harem forming or open polygamists.

Ectodinids: Possibly the most beautiful of Tanganyikan cichlids can be found within the tribe Ectodini. As far as an aquarist is concerned, this tribe is comprised of two very distinctive groups: the featherfins of the genera *Ophthalmotilapia*, *Cyathopharynx*, *Cunningtonia*, and related forms, and the sand-dwelling Xenotilapias and their allies. The featherfins are so named for the males' highly elongated ventral fins that frequently end in a small paddle-shaped egg dummy. These are midwater planktivores that practice open polygamy. Males create elaborate spawning pits or arenas and frequently assemble to form leks. In contrast, the remaining ectodinids inhabit areas with an open sandy substrate and are frequently found in large schools. They are maternal mouthbrooders, the eggs being first deposited in a sandy pit constructed by a dominant male. All the ectodinids are rather delicate and definitely not beginners' fish. They are exceedingly sensitive to dissolved metabolites, and do not compete well with more aggressive species.

Two other groups of Tanganyikan cichlids that have captured the fancy of aquarists, but have very different life styles and dispositions, belong to the genus *Tropheus* within the tribe Tropheini, and the cyprichromids of the genera *Cyprichromis* and *Paracyprichromis*.

Tropheus: *Tropheus* are highly aggressive, open polygamists that are intimately associated with rocky areas. In nature, algae comprises the bulk of their diet, and their aquarium diet should reflect their vegetarian nature. The various species of *Tropheus* can be thought of as the Tanganyikan equivalents of the Malawian mbunas. Like mbunas, many of these fish come in a bewildering number of distinctly colored geographical forms, some of which may prove to be distinct species. These fish do very well when kept in groups of one male and several females. Males are extremely aggressive toward each other and under no circumstances should more than a single male of any species be kept in the same aquarium. Males do not establish breeding territories, the spawning act occurring wherever a male encounters a receptive female. Their eggs are extremely large and few in number, and the large, well-developed fry are easily raised. Due to their aggressive nature *Tropheus* spp. should not be housed together with peaceful species such as *Xenotilapia*.

Cyprichromids: In sharp contrast are the exceedingly peaceful cyprichromids. These are school-forming, open-water micropredators that in nature feed upon pelagic zooplankton. Their aquariums should be large and roomy, with plenty of open swimming space. All cyprichromids are highly social species that should always be maintained in groups of at least six. It is also essential that aggressive species be banned from their aquarium. Males of a number of cyprichromid species do not establish a substrate-based breeding territory, but spawn in midwater. Egg fertilization is extrabuccal, the female snapping up the fertilized eggs as they fall through the water column. As with many Tanganyikan mouthbrooders, incubation lasts about 21 days. Adults ignore the newly released young, but the fry are rather delicate and require numerous small feedings daily and superb water quality if they are to thrive.

Lake Victoria

This second-largest lake in the world was once home to what has been estimated as more than 400 species of fish, most being endemic cichlids. This situation has dramatically changed for the worse since the 1970s when the Nile perch (*Lates nilotica*), a huge introduced predator, started eating its way through this lake's fish fauna. At present it is estimated that nearly half of Lake Victoria's fish species are extinct, with many others severely reduced in numbers. Obviously, there is no way to remove the Nile perch from this enormous lake, and we can only look on with sadness until a new equilibrium among the ultimately surviving species becomes established. By maintaining some of these fish in aquariums, hobbyists can do their part to ensure the survival of at least a few of these beautiful and interesting cichlids.

Just about all the Lake Victoria cichlids of interest to aquarists are haplochromines of small to medium size. They are easily maintained and bred, and significantly more adaptable to changing water conditions and dissolved metabolites than their Rift Lakes relatives. Preferred temperatures are 72–82°F (22–28°C), but they can tolerate short-term exposure to temperatures approaching 90°F (32°C). In addition, they are easily fed and tolerate a wide range of pH and water hardness, as long as extremes are avoided. All are openly polygamous maternal mouthbrooders with pronounced sexual dimorphism. Males are more brightly colored and display considerable aggression toward one another. When kept in mixed-species groups these cichlids frequently produce hybrids. It is therefore essential to breed them in single-species tanks. These fish possess great beauty and are highly endangered in nature. It is therefore unfortunate that they have not yet achieved as high a level of popularity within the hobby as their Malawi and Tanganyikan relatives.

Marlier's Julie, Julidochromis marlieri, *was one of the first Tanganyikan cichlids to enter the hobby.*

The shell-dwelling Neolamprologus brevis *is one of the smallest of Lake Tanganyikan cichlids.*

Ophthalmotilapia heterodontus *(male shown) is one of the fascinating and graceful species known as featherfins.*

The genus Cyprichromis *(C. sp. "karilani" shown here) are peaceful and rather delicate mid-water species that should be kept in groups.*

The beauty of Lake Victoria cichlids is well shown by these three species.

Above left: Pundamilia nyrerei *(male).*
Above right: Astatotilapia latifasciata *(male).*
Right: "Haplochromis" sp. "Kenya gold fulu."

Although in an aquarium with adequate rock structures and hiding places a reasonable percentage of mouthbrooding African cichlid fry stand a good chance of surviving, there are still times when it might be advisable to catch the brooding female and strip the developing embryos from her mouth for artificial incubation and subsequent raising within a separate nursery aquarium.

When to Use Artificial Incubation

For instance, the fish might have spawned in a community aquarium that also contains species that are particularly efficient predators of baby fish, or you

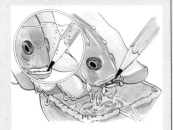

With wet hands, gently hold the brooding female in one hand. With a pencil in the other, carefully pry open its mouth over the parents' aquarium with a net in place. After the juveniles have been released from the female's mouth, the babies can be transferred to a grow-out aquarium.

might feel that it would be difficult to provide enough food for the fry in a community setting. You might also have spawned a particularly desirable and rare species and, therefore, wish to raise as many young as possible, or the aquarium in which the spawning occurred is a bit overcrowded and would not provide enough room for additional fish.

The Process of Artificial Incubation

For all of the above reasons it is a good idea for you as an aquarist to be familiar with the techniques involved in removing a brooding female from her aquarium, stripping the developing embryos from her mouth, and then incubating them artificially. To do this successfully is not difficult, but it takes a bit of practice. It is most successful when the developing young are stripped as close as possible to the end of their incubation period (when they are virtually free-swimming and will not require special care). This requires that you note the day that your fish spawned and are familiar with the incubation period for the species in question. If you estimate incorrectly and the young are only partially

developed, you will have to construct an "artificial mouth" that will keep the embryos in a state of constant mild agitation that mimics the tumbling action they experience in their mother's mouth. One way of doing this is to suspend a cylindrical plastic container within the nursery aquarium. For ease of observation this container should be transparent. A one-liter or smaller soda bottle works well. Simply cut the bottom from the bottle, invert it, and cap it in a manner similar to that used when constructing a brine shrimp hatcher (see page 63). A simple flotation collar can be made from a section of Styrofoam in which you cut a circular opening a tiny bit smaller in diameter than the plastic bottle. The Styrofoam collar is then forced over the inverted bottle's cut end and will stay in place due to friction. A few small, smooth-edged holes should be made in the walls of this container to permit free interchange of water between the container and the aquarium, but they should not be large enough for the eggs to fall through. An air line or piece of tubing attached to a small water pump is inserted all the way to the bottom of the floating

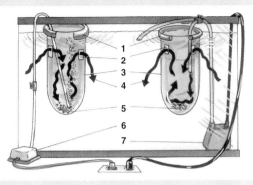

Two types of artificial
incubators for mouthbrooding
cichlid eggs.

1. flotation device
2. vents
3. inverted plastic soda bottle
4. water current
5. embryo eggs
6. air pump
7. water pump

container and adjusted until it creates just enough water movement to keep the eggs constantly agitated. Once the embryos' yolk sacs are absorbed and they become free-swimming, they should be released within the nursery tank. If you have been using a water pump to provide the water movement during incubation, it should now be removed in order to prevent the fry from being sucked into the pump.

Catching a Brooding Female

It is simplest to catch the brooding female with the aid of a flashlight when she is asleep at night. There are several ways to remove the eggs from her mouth. The method most frequently used for larger species is as follows.

✔ While holding the fish in a wet fish net, gently open her mouth with a smooth instrument, such as a blunt pencil.

✔ With her mouth held open, position her head-down over a net with her head below the water's surface. Whether the fish is holding eggs or well-developed fry, they should quickly fall or swim into the net.

A recommended technique for smaller, fragile species involves the use of a kitchen meat baster.

✔ First remove the bulb from the tube and then place the brooding female head-down within the tube.

✔ Replace the bulb and hold the baster partly submerged in water for a minute or two.

✔ Next, remove the baster from the water for one to two minutes before replacing it in the water while squeezing the bulb briskly a few times. If the young are not released on the first try the procedure can be repeated until success is achieved. Although this might sound like a rough procedure, it is really quite gentle on the fish and minimizes the chances of injury.

These same procedures can be used for most maternal or paternal mouthbrooding cichlids from other regions of the world, although some South American mouthbrooders may spit out the eggs or fry when an attempt is made to net the brooding parent. After the female has been stripped of her young she can be placed back in her original aquarium.

Note: The nursery aquarium should be large enough to comfortably house a growing brood of young cichlids and filled with water of the same temperature and chemical makeup as the tank the fish had spawned in. A well-cycled sponge filter should suffice as a source of biological and mechanical filtration without any chance of it sucking in the fry.

CICHLIDS OF MADAGASCAR AND ASIA

It might seem odd to group the cichlids of Madagascar with those of Asia. However, even though the island of Madagascar is located off southeastern Africa, its cichlid fauna is more closely allied to that of the Indian subcontinent than to that of Africa.

Malagasy Cichlids

The exact number of cichlids indigenous to Madagascar is not fully known but probably numbers between 25 and 30. The situation is complicated by widespread environmental destruction and the introduction of numerous exotic fish species, both of which have caused the extinction or critical endangerment of the native fish fauna. It is probable that some Malagasy cichlids have, or will, become extinct before their discovery by science.

Madagascar cichlids have only recently been introduced into the hobby. All are easily satisfied and adaptable to a wide range of pH and hardness. As Dr. Paul Loiselle, the well-known authority on these and other cichlids, explained to me, their only requirement is that their water "be wet." A temperature of 75–85°F

*A pair of green chromides, **Etroplus suratensis**, cleaning a potential spawning site.*

(24–29°C) suits them well, with the warmer end of this range conducive to spawning. These are rather large cichlids that require roomy accommodations.

Paratilapias: At the time of this writing (2001), the only species that can be considered common in the hobby are *Paratilapia polleni* and *P. bleekeri* (see page 92). These are both strikingly beautiful fish covered with numerous metallic spangles over an almost black ground color. In nature they can grow to over 12 inches (30 cm) but normally remain smaller in an aquarium. For such large cichlids these two species are remarkably tolerant of other species, becoming distinctly aggressive only during periods of heightened sexual activity. Males are more brightly colored, larger, and more "bull-headed" than females, and develop longer tips to their dorsal and anal fins. Paratilapias are generalized carnivores with a piscivorous tendency. Aquarium specimens have hearty appetites and will accept most frozen

Cichlid Habitats of Madagascar

Listed below are the habitats of cichlids native to Madagascar and their location within the identified habitats.

Habitat	Location Within
Lake Andrapongy	Anjingo River System
coastal streams	Canal de Pangalanes
Hernandrano River	Hernandrano River System
near Marolambo	Nosivolo River System
Hanana River	Onilahy River System
near Mandritsara	Sofia River System

and even dry foods of suitable size. Chopped minnows, small shrimp, and other "meaty" foods are particularly relished.

Both of these Paratilapias are biparentally custodial substrate spawners that are capable of producing spawns in excess of 3,000 eggs that at 82°F (28°C) take two days to hatch. The young become free-swimming after an additional four days and are large enough to accept brine shrimp nauplii.

Paretroplus and Ptychochromis: Several other attractive Malagasy cichlids of the genera *Paretroplus* and *Ptychochromis* (see page 93) are now being bred commercially and it is sincerely hoped that they develop an enthusiastic following within the hobby. As far as is known, all are open substrate spawners. Experts at zoological institutions and hobbyists who are maintaining these fish claim that breeding adults can be extremely aggressive toward both their own kind and other species. Biologists studying *Paretroplus* in nature indicate that they are highly vegetarian, consuming leaves and bulbs of aquatic plants, while *Ptychochromis* are more generalized invertebrate feeders. Both genera have proven easily fed, but it is suggested that the diet of *Paretroplus* spp. include adequate vegetable matter.

Similar to the situation in Lake Victoria, the future of the Malagasy cichlid fauna is far from encouraging. Dedicated aquarists can do much to increase our knowledge of the biology of these unique fish, as well as help in preventing their total extinction.

Asian Cichlids

The cichlids of Asia are few in number, being limited to three species belonging to the genus *Etroplus* that inhabit the southern portions of the Indian subcontinent and the island of Sri Lanka. Only two of these have entered the aquarium hobby, the green chromide (see page 87), *E. suratensis*, and the orange chromide, *E. maculatus* (see page 92). The orange chromide is definitely the more popular of the two, especially the xanthistic orange mutation. The green chromide is considerably the larger, reaching a length of 10 inches (25 cm) in nature, and about three-quarters that length in captivity. In contrast, the orange chromide rarely exceeds 3 inches (8 cm). Both chromides are very peaceful as far as cichlids go and do well in community aquariums with fish of similar size.

These cichlids are native to lowland fresh and brackish waters, and prefer hard and alkaline aquarium conditions. The green chromide is particularly fussy in this respect and appreciates the addition of some sea salt to its water. In nature these two fish live together and have developed a unique relationship. The orange chromide feeds upon the eggs of its relative, but young orange chromides pick and consume ectoparasites from the skin of the green chromide in a behavior reminiscent of the well-known marine cleaner wrasses. Coming from southern India, both require warmth and should be maintained at close to 80°F (27°C), a few degrees warmer for breeding. While the

Cichlids of Asia

Asia is home to only three species of cichlids. They are found in the southern portions of India and the island of Sri Lanka.

green chromide is highly herbivorous and devours most aquarium plants, the orange chromide ignores all but the most tender plants and looks its best in a planted aquarium. Another difference between the two is that while the orange chromide is a biparentally custodial cave spawner, the green chromide lays its eggs on an exposed substrate, frequently preferring one that is vertically oriented. When kept in conditions to its liking, the orange chromide is among the most easily bred of cichlids. Its larger cousin is definitely a much greater challenge to spawn. It is best not to separate green chromide young from their parents too early, as the young fry feed partly on the mucus of their parents, reminiscent of the South American discus and uaru.

INFORMATION

Abbreviations, Equivalents, and Conversions

Abbreviations
Celsius or centigrade (°C)
centimeters (cm)
Fahrenheit (°F)
grams (g)
kilograms (kg)
liters (L)
meters (m)
millimeters (mm)
milliliters (ml)
parts per million (ppm)

Equivalents
one centimeter equals 10 millimeters
one foot equals 12 inches
one gallon equals 32 ounces
one gallon equals 4 quarts
one kilogram equals 1,000 grams
one meter equals 1,000 millimeters
one tablespoon equals 3 teaspoons

Conversions

Measurement	Multiplied by	Equals
centimeters	0.4	inches
inches	2.54	centimeters
feet	30.0	centimeters
grams	0.035	ounces
liters	1.06	quarts
millimeters	0.04	inches
pounds	0.45	kilograms
quarts	0.95	liters
teaspoons	5.0	milliliters

Temperature Conversions:
Multiply °Celsius by 1.8 and add 32 to obtain °Fahrenheit.

Subtract 32 from °Fahrenheit and multipy this by 0.55 to obtain °Celsius.

Top: The easily spawned orange chromide, Etroplus maculatus, has long been a popular aquarium fish. The orange mutational form is shown.

Bottom: Paratilapia bleekeri, shown here, and its relative P. polleni are the only Malagasy cichlids that are well established in the hobby.

Useful Literature

Magazines
Aquarium Fish
Fancy Publications, Inc.
Subscription Department
P.O. Box 53351
Boulder, CO 80323-3351

Cichlid News
Aquatic Promotions, Inc.
P.O. Box 522842
Miami, FL 33152

Freshwater and Marine Aquarium
144 West Sierra Madre Boulevard
Sierra Madre, CA 91024

Tropical Fish Hobbyist
TFH Publications, Inc.
211 West Sylvania Avenue
Neptune, NJ 07753

Books
Fairfield, Terry. *A Commonsense Guide to Fish Health.* Hauppauge, NY: Barron's Educational Series, Inc., 2000.
Liebel, Dr. Wayne S. *A Fishkeeper's Guide to South American Cichlids.* Blacksburg, VA: Tetra Press, 1993.
Linke, Horst, and Dr. Wolfgang Staeck. *American Cichlids I: Dwarf Cichlids; Handbook for Their Identification, Care and Breeding.* Blacksburg, VA: Tetra Press, 1994.
Loiselle, Dr. Paul V. *The Cichlid Aquarium.* Blacksburg, VA: Tetra Press, 1994.
____. *A Fishkeeper's Guide to African Cichlids.* Blacksburg, VA: Tetra Press, 1988.
Noga, Edward J. *Fish Disease, Diagnosis and Treatment.* St. Louis, MO: Mosby, 1996.
Smith, Mark. *Lake Malawi Cichlids: A Complete Pet Owner's Manual.* Hauppauge, NY: Barron's Educational Series, Inc., 2000.
____. *Lake Tanganyika Cichlids: A Complete Pet Owner's Manual.* Hauppauge, NY: Barron's Educational Series, Inc., 1998.
____. *Lake Victoria Basin Cichlids: A Complete Pet Owner's Manual.* Hauppauge, NY: Barron's Educational Series, Inc., 2001.
Untergasser, Dieter. *Handbook of Fish Diseases.* Neptune City, NJ: TFH Publications, Inc., 1989.

Organizations
American Cichlid Association
ACA Membership
P.O. Box 361115
Decatur, GA 30036-1115
http://www.cichlid.org

Deutsche Cichliden Gesellschaft
Parkstrasse 21a
D-33719 Bielfeld
Germany

British Cichlid Association
248 Longridge, Knutsford
Cheshire, WA18 8PH
England

Ptychochromis grandidieri *is known in Madagascar as the Saroy.*

About the Author

Georg Zurlo is a teacher who has been keeping fish for many years. He is the author of many articles. Cichlids of the New and Old World are his field of special interest.

Photo Credits

Nature's Images: pages 2–3, 4, 9, 12 top left, 12 top right, 12 bottom left, 13 top left, 13 top right, 13 bottom right, 17, 21, 25, 28 top left, 28 top right, 28 bottom left, 28 bottom right, 33, 36 middle, 37 top left, 37 top right, 37 bottom, 40, 41, 44 top left, 44 top right, 44 middle right, 44 bottom left, 44 bottom right, 45 top left, 45 top right, 48, 49, 53, 56 bottom right, 57 top, 60 top left, 60 bottom left, 60 bottom right, 61 bottom left, 65, 68 top left, 73, 81 top left, 88, 89, 92 bottom left; Mark Smith: pages 5, 12 bottom right, 13 middle right, 32, 36 bottom, 56 top left, 76 bottom left, 77 top left, 77 top right, 80 top left, 81 top right, 81 bottom, 84 bottom, 85 top, 92 top left; Linke: pages 8, 16, 52; Kahl: pages 36 top, 56 bottom right, 61 bottom right, 72, 84 top left, 84 top right; Werner: page 45 bottom, 69; Dr. Paul V. Loiselle: pages 60 middle left, 61 top left, 76 top left, 84 middle left, 85 middle left, 85 bottom, 93; Stawikovski: pages 61 top right, 68 bottom left, 80 top right; Meulengracht-Madson/Biofoto: page 64.

Cover Credits

Front Cover: Nature's Images (*Astronotus ocellatus*); Inside Front Cover: Mark Smith (Synodontis *multipunctatus*); Inside Back Cover: Mark Smith (*Metriaclima lombardoi*); Back Cover: Mark Smith (*Copadichromis cf. azureus*).

Important Note

In this book, electrical equipment commonly used with aquariums is described. Please be sure to observe manufacturers' directions and rules of safety; otherwise there is a danger of serious accidents.

Before buying a large tank, check how much weight the floor of your home or apartment can support in the location where you plan to set up your aquarium.

Sometimes water damage occurs as a result of broken glass, overflowing, or a leak in the tank. An insurance policy that covers such eventualities is therefore highly recommended.

Make sure that adults, children, or pets do not eat any aquarium plants. These plants can make people and animals quite sick. Also make sure that fish medications are out of reach of children.

About the Revising Author

Dr. David M. Schleser has been a hobbyist for over 45 years and served for over 5 years as Curator/Aquatic Biologist for the Dallas Aquarium in Texas. At present, he works full time for Nature's Images, Inc., a natural history photography and writing company that he helped establish. Since 1993, Dr. Schleser has led ecological and tropical fish study and collecting trips to the Peruvian Amazon. He is also the author of two aquarium fish books published by Barron's Educational Series, Inc. and lectures widely throughout the United States and Canada.

English translation © Copyright 2002, 1991 by Barron's Educational Series, Inc.

Original title of the book in German is *Buntbarche Cichliden*

© Copyright 1990 by Gräfe und Unzer, Verlag GmbH, Munich

All inquiries should be addressed to:
Barron's Educational Series, Inc.
250 Wireless Boulevard
Hauppauge, NY 11788
http://www.barronseduc.com

International Standard Book No. 0-7641-1956-7
Library of Congress Catalog Card No. 2001052587

Library of Congress Cataloging-in-Publication Data
Zurlo, Georg.
    [Buntbarsche Cichliden. English]
    Cichlids : a complete pet owner's manual : everything about purchase, care, nutrition, behavior, and training / Georg Zurlo ; as revised by David M. Schleser.—2nd ed.
        p. cm.
    ISBN 0-7641-1956-7 (alk. paper)
    1. Cichlids. 2. Aquarium fishes. I. Schleser, David M. II. Title.
SF458.C5 Z8713 2002
639.3'774—dc21   2001052587

Printed in Hong Kong
9 8 7 6 5 4